THE BOY BILLIONAIRE

D1026279

THE BOY BILLIONAIRE

Mark Zuckerberg In His Own Words

EDITED BY GEORGE BEAHM

AN AGATE IMPRINT

CHICAGO

Library of Congress Cataloging-in-Publication Data

The boy billionaire : Mark Zuckerberg in his own words / edited by
George Beahm.
    pages cm
  Includes bibliographical references and index.
  Summary: "A collection of direct quotes from Mark Zuckerberg on
topics related to business, technology, social media, and life collected
from his own speeches, interviews, and writings"--Provided by pub-
lisher.
  ISBN 978-1-932841-76-3 (pbk.) -- ISBN 1-932841-76-8 (pbk.)
  1. Zuckerberg, Mark, 1984- 2. Zuckerberg, Mark, 1984---Quotations.
3. Businesspeople--Quotations. 4. Social media--Quotations, max-
ims, etc. I. Zuckerberg, Mark, 1984- II. Beahm, George W.
  HM479.Z83B69 2012
  006.7092--dc23

                            2012043246

10 9 8 7 6 5 4 3 2 1

B2 is an imprint of Agate Publishing. Agate books are available in
bulk at discount prices. For more information, go to
agatepublishing.com.

This one is for "The Boys."

Facebook was not originally created to build a company. It was built to accomplish a social mission—to make the world open and more connected. . . . We don't build services in order to make money; we make money to build better services.

—MARK ZUCKERBERG

TABLE OF CONTENTS

NET WORTH: THE BOY BILLIONAIRE......................**15**

QUOTATIONS BY MARK ZUCKERBERG **31**

Personal.. **33**

Being Robbed...35

Eliminating Desire...35

Advice to Students: Get With the Program...........35

Google+ Profile 36

Getting Zucked 36

Death Sentence..36

Speaking Mandarin..37

Embracing *The Lord of the Flies*.......................37

Focus and Simplicity.......................................38

Zuckerberg's Likes 38

College **39**

Mindset 42

Animal Farm...42

No Job 43

HarvardConnection...43

Hacking for the Fun of It..................................44

Building Thefacebook 45

Zuckerberg's Initial Debt 45

Code Monkey..46

Backing Out of HarvardConnection.............46

Psychology + CS = Facebook.............47

Maturation.............47

Facebook's Origin.............48

Jettisoning Eduardo Saverin.............48

Stock Dilution of Saverin's Shares.............49

Starting Out.............51

Silicon Valley's Culture.............53

Location, Location, Location.............53

Silicon Valley's Short-Term Vision.............54

Dumb Mistakes.............54

MySpace and Facebook: Cool vs. Useful.............56

Facebook.............57

Mission-Oriented.............57

Independence.............57

Corporate Culture.............58

Board, Not Bored, Meetings.............59

Core Desire.............59

Core Principles.............60

Reach.............60

Education.............61

Goals.............61

Instagram.............62

Lawyers.............62

Mobile Platforms.............62

News Feed.............63

In Touch.............63

Online Directory.............64

Openness 65

People-Centric 65

Connecting 65

Information Control 66

Sharing 66

Privacy 67

Privacy Settings 67

Privacy Tools 68

Privacy from Day One 68

Sharing Information 69

Self-Revelations 70

Information Conduit 70

Virtual Friends, Virtually Forever 70

The Super Power of Word of Mouth 71

Lawsuits 73

Every Capitalist 75

I Fought the Law and the Law Won 76

Big Brother Is Watching 77

The Social Network **79**

The Social Network 80

The Social Network's Depiction

   of Zuckerberg 80

The Social Network's Positive Aspects 81

Mission 83

Ubiquity 84

Long-Range Vision 84

Steve Jobs 88

Process...87

Product Improvement.................................87

On Innovation 88

On Focus..88

Social Context and Serendipity 89

First Things First...................................... 89

Fast Movers 89

The Hacker's Way................................... 90

Hacking's Good...................................... 90

Hackathons 91

Values...93

No Games..93

Making Mistakes 94

Getting Things Done 94

Siding with the Underdog........................ 94

Caring...95

Users' Privacy Controls 95

Entrepreneur/CEO 95

Not Selling Out 96

Employees' Leverage 98

The Power of Focus................................. 98

Creating Value....................................... 99

Employees Growing on the Job................ 99

Measuring Value 100

Building Companies................................ 101

Facebook's Biggest Challenges 101

Prioritizing 102

Hiring Employees 102

Motivation..103

The Next Big Thing...103

Fast and Faster...104

Selling Out..104

Accountability 105

Stepping In It and Scraping It Off..........................106

On FTC Allegations of Privacy Violations..........106

Vision 107

SOPA (Stop Online Piracy) and PIPA (Protect
    Intellectual Property Act)....................................107

A Blinding Flash of the Obvious 107

On the Future of Email...108

Risk-Taking 108

Facebook's Future..109

Social Trending 109

The Evolution of Mass
    Communication Tools...110

Responsible Governments 110

A Social Web...111

Responsibilities 111

Information Sharing 111

Companies Admired..112

Transparency in History...112

Monetizing: Cash In by Cashing Out....................113

The Web's Future 113

On the Future of Social Networking.....................114

Philanthropy **115**
Early Philanthropy.. 115
Organ Donations 115
The Power of Friends....................................... 116

MARK ZUCKERBERG'S LETTER TO INVESTORS 117

MILESTONES.. 129

RECOMMENDED RESOURCES 137

CITATIONS 141

ENDNOTES 169

ABOUT THE EDITOR...................................... 171

NET WORTH: THE BOY BILLIONAIRE

A t 9:30 a.m. Eastern Standard Time, on May 18, 2012, surrounded by Facebook employees behind a makeshift NASDAQ podium in Menlo Park, California, Mark Zuckerberg rang the NASDAQ's opening bell to signal the beginning of the trading day in New York. It was just four days after his 28th birthday, eight scant years after he originally conceived the idea of Facebook as a Harvard sophomore in his dormitory room, and the first day Facebook shares were traded publicly.

Facebook's long-awaited IPO raised $16 billion, giving it a market valuation of $104 billion. It made Zuckerberg one of the world's youngest billionaires. The following day, he married his long-time girlfriend, Priscilla Chan, and the next chapter of his life began.

***

Walt Disney famously said, "I don't make movies to make money; I make money to make movies."

It's a working philosophy that Mark Zuckerberg clearly espouses in his letter that accompanies Facebook's Form S-1 Registration Statement: "We don't build services to make money; we make money to build better services."

This is a viewpoint that's at odds with most, if not all, entrepreneurs in Silicon Valley, where the goal is to create an app or a website, generate maximum demand for the product, and then sell out for megabucks as quickly as possible. But that doesn't seem to be Zuckerberg's mindset. In fact, when Microsoft approached him in 2007 to buy out Facebook for $15 billion, Zuckerberg politely declined.

It's a viewpoint that perplexes many in the tech industry and business community. In retrospect, of course, Zuckerberg made more money waiting until he could launch his IPO. But how many dot-com founders would have done the same?

For the ordinary person with bills to pay, the idea of refusing billions of dollars is inconceivable. In fact, when David Kirkpatrick, author of *The Facebook Effect*, fields questions from his readers, the issue of money is of principal concern. As he told an interviewer for the Computer History Museum, "People have a really hard time believing that about Facebook. That's a fact. … It's one aspect of my book that people challenge me on everywhere I go. They cannot believe that Facebook isn't doing it for the money, for the ad marketplace, etc."

The Early Years

Early on, it was clear to everyone that Mark Elliot Zuckerberg was special. The only son of Edward and Karen Zuckerberg, who also have three daughters, Mark was born in White Plains, New York, on May 14, 1984. (Coincidentally, it's the same year Apple Computer released its revolutionary Mac computer.)

Mark, as his father noted in the 2010 *Time* article which named Mark the Person of the Year, has always been intellectually demanding, even as a child. As Dr. Zuckerberg explained, if his son asked a question and the answer was "yes," no further elaboration was required; but a "no" required an explanation that had to be vigorously defended. Mark's interrogative ways might have suggested that they had a budding lawyer on their hands. It was a logical assumption, but their son's interests lay elsewhere: specifically, in the binary world of computer science.

At an early age, Mark's penchant for computers was obvious: at age 12, using Atari BASIC, he wrote a software program for messaging that was used at home and also at his father's dental practice. Called "Zucknet," it was the first "Mark Zuckerberg production"—a tagline that would originally run across the bottom of the early iterations of Zuckerberg's social media platform.

When his parents noticed their son's consuming interest in computer science, they hired a tutor—a software developer named David Newman who quickly realized that Mark was not your typical student but in fact a prodigy. Supplementing these lessons, Mark Zuckerberg also took a class in BASIC programming at nearby Mercy College. (When Dr. Zuckerberg took his son to school, he was told by the instructor that his son couldn't accompany him to class. Dr. Zuckerberg explained that Mark was the student, and not himself.)

Mark then transferred from Ardsley High School to a prestigious prep school, Phillips Exeter Academy (Exeter, New Hampshire), principally because it had a more robust computer science curriculum.

Even in sports, Zuckerberg seems to favor brains over brawn. At Phillips Exeter he starting fencing, a sport that requires intense focus, quick reflexes, and hand-eye coordination. He went on to become captain of the fencing team.

He also developed a software application called Synapse, similar to Pandora. It attracted interest from Microsoft and AOL, resulting in offers to buy. Turning them down, Zuckerberg subsequently gave away the software for free.

Harvard

Zuckerberg entered Harvard as a freshman in fall 2002.

At first glance, given his obvious talent for computer science, nearby MIT (Massachusetts Institute of Technology) would seem a more suitable fit for Zuckerberg. Harvard, however, offered a more rounded curriculum, and he also had an interest in psychology—not surprising, since his mother is a former psychiatrist.

By Zuckerberg's sophomore year, he had earned a reputation as a computer geek after posting CourseMatch online, which allowed students to see who was taking what courses.

As for Zuckerberg's personal life, he began dating Priscilla Chan, whom he would later marry in 2012.

Though CourseMatch brought Zuckerberg to the attention of his peers, it was his next project that put him on the radar of the Harvard community at large. To help with student identification, Harvard posted online directories of photographs called "Facebooks," individual mug shots of the student body.

After hacking into the official Facebooks, Zuckerberg built a program called "Facemash" that posted photos of female students side by side, requiring the user to judge whom was "hotter."

Wildly popular among his peers, the website drew outrage and calls to bring down the site from many groups on campus who vociferously complained to the administration. The site was shut down after only four hours of operation. It earned the puckish Zuckerberg an administrative hearing, after which he had to see a counselor.

What most people didn't know was that Harvard's students had gotten off comparatively easy: His original idea had been to post their photos with farm animals to judge the more attractive of the two. Zuckerberg abandoned that idea quickly, though, and ratcheted down to the slightly less offensive website idea.

The short-lived site firmly cemented Zuckerberg's reputation as the go-to guy for computer coding. It was then that he drew the attention of three upperclassmen who were developing a dating website exclusively for the Harvard community called HarvardConnection. Divya Narendra and twins Cameron and Tyler Winklevoss were looking to recruit a computer geek to quickly write code for their fledgling website. Time, they realized, was of the essence; they wanted to capitalize on having first-mover advantage. After seeing what Zuckerberg had done with Facemash, they realized they had found their man—or so they thought.

Zuckerberg agreed to work on the project, but he quickly put it on the backburner in favor of his own projects. After repeated queries that inevitably met with frustration due to Zuckerberg's delaying tactics, the HarvardConnection team realized that his priorities weren't aligned with theirs. Zuckerberg had moved on to other interests and intentionally disconnected from HarvardConnection.

What displaced Zuckerberg's interest in HarvardConnection was his own social networking site called Thefacebook. Ensconced in Suite H33 at the Kirkland House dormitory, Zuckerberg and three colleagues worked in secrecy on the project. On January 11, 2004, they registered a domain, thefacebook.com, via register.com. It would be exclusively open to Harvard students with an email suffix of harvard.edu.

On February 4, 2004, Thefacebook went live, and Mark Zuckerberg's world was forever changed.

Janus

There's a classic *New Yorker* cartoon depicting a dog in front of a computer who says to another dog, "On the Internet, nobody knows you're a dog."[1] The Internet allows users to cloak themselves in anonymity, potentially fostering irresponsible or antisocial behavior such as stalking; posting libelous comments; initiating flame wars; and posting gratuitous, ugly, or racist comments.

To Zuckerberg, the dishonesty inherent in online anonymity was a major impediment to building a trusted community of online users. Requiring users to provide their actual email addresses, insured transparency and reassured users, especially women.

The secret sauce that Zuckerberg added to the mix was the element of transparency. On Thefacebook, the use of registered users' actual email addresses reassured users, especially women.

The two-faced Roman god Janus comes to mind. Janus, who could simultaneously look at the past and the future, is a fitting symbol for Zuckerberg, who looked at the history of social networking online and saw that it would have no future if the web community remained in the dark ages by staying anonymous.

Moreover, Zuckerberg must have found it difficult to serve two increasingly demanding taskmasters: an academic course load as an undergrad, and Thefacebook, which was becoming his principal interest.

Words of Wisdom

In a significant, life-changing moment, chronicled in Ben Mezrich's marvelously inventive look at Facebook, *The Accidental Billionaires*, Microsoft's Bill Gates spoke to a gathering of students on campus. "After hemming and hawing a bit, Gates told the audience that the great thing about Harvard was that you could always come back and finish," wrote Mezrich.

The idea must have made sense to Zuckerberg, who could see it as giving him a fail-safe option for Facebook. If he left Harvard and made the fledgling website succeed, fine; but if he left and Facebook failed, he could always return to the crimson fold of Harvard, finish his education, and get a well-paying job.

In June 2004 Mark Zuckerberg pulled the trigger. He left school and moved to Silicon Valley to work exclusively on Facebook. Facebook then had a solid base of over a million users, with the sky as the limit in terms of its potential.

Facebook's early success drew a lot of attention—especially from the Winklevoss twins, who filed a lawsuit in 2004 claiming copyright infringement. They contended that Mark Zuckerberg had clearly and brazenly stolen the basic idea of Facebook from them, and they were out to collect payment for the injustice.

The bitterly contested lawsuit, *Facebook, Inc. v. ConnectU, Inc.*, was initially dismissed, but ConnectU refiled, and the suit was eventually settled. Facebook paid an estimated $65 million in cash and stock shares. It was only afterward that incendiary instant messages by Zuckerberg surfaced. As Tyler Winklevoss told CNN's Piers Morgan in a February 8, 2011, interview, "At the time we settled, we had nowhere near the evidence that actually exists today. So we knew something had been done wrong. But what Facebook did throughout the entire litigation was suppress and withhold all the smoking gun electronic communications of Mark Zuckerberg."

Actually, the "smoking gun" was more of a misfire, according to *New Yorker* writer Jose Antonio Vargas. In "The Face of Facebook: Mark Zuckerberg Opens Up" (September 20, 2010), Vargas wrote, "Although the IMs did not offer any evidence to support the claim of theft, according to sources who have seen many of the messages, the IMs portray Zuckerberg as backstabbing, conniving, and insensitive."

The legal proceedings proved to be a distraction for Facebook and Zuckerberg, who had always proclaimed his innocence. To his way of thinking, Facebook and HarvardConnection were both social networking sites, but had little else in common. Zuckerberg asserted that the execution of the idea, and not the idea itself, was the essential difference, and he argued that his was the more popular website because it was simply more useful and embraced a larger virtual community.

Master of His Domain

When California witnessed a gold rush in 1848, hundreds of thousands of people were driven to seek their fame and fortune. California's current gold rush is found not in creek beds and gold nuggets, but in common sand—specifically, in silicon. Silicon Valley is a technological and financial epicenter located south of San Francisco. Financial angels, also known as venture capitalists, keep Silicon Valley alive by funding the dot-com dreams of hopeful entrepreneurs.

In 2004 Mark Zuckerberg and his friends moved to Palo Alto and rented a ranch-style house that served as both their personal residence and the office of the fledgling website. (They would later move into a nearby office building.) It was a modest beginning for what would be one of the biggest dot-coms of all time.

A year later, "Facebook was still just another smart ambitious startup," noted Tomio Geron in a 2012 piece for Forbes.com, "The Untold Story of Two Early Facebook Investors." Facebook, he noted, had only 10 employees at that time.

Thefacebook got its jump-start when Zuckerberg appeared on a panel to discuss entrepreneurialism and startups at Stanford University, along with venture capitalist and Paypal cofounder Peter

Thiel, entrepreneur Sean Parker, and venture capitalist Venky Harinarayan of Cambrian Ventures.

It was Harinarayan who told *Forbes* magazine, "The thing that surprised me the most was there were over 700 people in the audience. I've never seen so many people in one place at Stanford. Folks there were so passionate about Facebook I was absolutely stunned. ... I remember talking to Accel [an investment firm] after. The key reason they invested was because they talked to Stanford students and found out that they use Facebook for two hours a day."

In May 2005 Harinarayan and his partner Anand Rajaraman invested in Facebook (by this time Parker had recommended shortening from "Thefacebook"). Going in with Accel, the investment was to the tune of $12.7 million—sweet music to Zuckerberg's ears. Now his company had sufficient operating capital to properly launch the company and position it for significant future growth. Up until then, Facebook's reach had been deliberately restricted to a handful of universities, but when it opened up to other colleges and high schools both in the United States and abroad, the company soon attracted 5.5 million users. It was December 2005, and Facebook's rapid growth captured the attention of larger companies looking to acquire potentially lucrative dot-coms.

For the next seven years, Facebook fended off suitors as it continued to increase its user base, expand its products and services, and build momentum for its eventual IPO.

During that time, Facebook needed money, and a lot of it, because of the increasing demand for computer servers and support infrastructure. Despite the pressures from third-party companies who wooed Zuckerberg, he remained steadfast. Facebook was not for sale because it was positioning itself for its eventual IPO.

Facebook's IPO

According to *Forbes* (May 2012), Facebook's IPO, on May 18, 2012, was the third largest in history, eclipsed only by Visa and Enel (a power company). Early investors had a lot to smile about during Facebook's IPO, though their joy didn't last long because as of this writing (November 2012), Facebook's stock is worth half its original price—$19.50 per share, down from $38.[2]

Zuckerberg didn't speak publicly about the IPO for months. "Painful," was eventually his first comment regarding the stock's drop, during a mid-August 2012 staff meeting. The worst, though, may be yet to come. When companies go public, there is often a lockup period that prevents company insiders and majority stakeholders from trading for a period of time after the IPO. On November 12, when many significant lockups for Facebook expire, an estimated 1.2 billion shares may go on the market. The impact that this will have on the stock price remains to be seen.

In time, its stock may rise, but currently, Facebook is having to dig itself out of a very deep hole of its own making. Before the IPO, insiders said there were too many shares, and they were also overpriced. In hindsight, although the canaries in the mine sounded the alarm, Facebook and investors alike did not heed their warning.

"Stay Focused & Keep Shipping"

Zuckerberg's mantra, "stay focused and keep shipping," has served Facebook well, through both growth years and lean years. He posted the motivational sign on Facebook's walls at corporate headquarters prior to the IPO; he didn't want the IPO to distract employees from their continuing mission at hand—"to give people the power to share and make the world more open and connected."[3]

That must now be Facebook's continued focus. The company is now at a crossroads and must fend for itself in a larger world and answer to anxious stockholders who hold sizable investments in the company.

This is a time when users are increasingly shifting to mobile devices, requiring Facebook to retool. Where its users go, so too must Facebook. Their numbers are the fuel that keeps Facebook's engine revved up, moving forward. It's *all* about the numbers, inextricably linked to the ad-based revenue on which Facebook's future rests.

As for what the future holds for Facebook, none can say. A company in flux, Facebook continues to forge on with new products in the works, while Wall Street looks on nervously and wonders if the stock will recover and, in a best-case scenario, rise and become profitable.

It's a turbulent time, so what's a CEO to do?

Mark Zuckerberg must remain calm, man the helm, and steer to safe harbor. He's in a perfect storm that, ironically, is of his own making.

QUOTATIONS BY MARK ZUCKERBERG

Even before Facebook's IPO, Mark Zuckerberg was a media magnet. Predictably, many of the profiles and feature articles focused on his youthfulness, his personality quirks, and, most often, his wealth—in short, his celebrity.

It doesn't help that Zuckerberg seems to be a very private person, as he rarely gives interviews. As the principal founder of Facebook and its current CEO, however, interviews and public pronouncements are expected, and so he reluctantly steps into the limelight. He'd prefer to hang out with his friends, who call him "Zuck;" or with his new wife, Dr. Priscilla Chan; or with his parents in Dobbs Ferry, New York; or with his three sisters who are scattered across the United States.

It all started in a small dorm room at Harvard, back in 2004, when he posted Thefacebook online. Building and running the most successful social networking site in the world became his life's work. In 2012 Facebook hit 1 billion users—not bad for a college dropout.

Rightly characterized as the face of Facebook, Zuckerberg is also its heart and soul. It'd be hard to imagine Facebook without Mark Zuckerberg, though some investors have floated that idea in the wake of its depressed stock price.

In this section, we will see what he sees through his own eyes—not filtered through a public relations flack, an official spokesperson, an authorized representative, or a media contact.

PERSONAL

Unlike the late Steve Jobs, Mark Zuckerberg shies away from the limelight and the cameras. But insights into Zuckerberg's personal life reveal a lot about his character, about how he thinks, and about his values that have shaped Facebook.

For those whose perceptions of him principally rely on the film *The Social Network* and the book that it's based on, he's seen as smart, cocky, abrupt, supercilious, and a world-class jerk. Ben Mezrich, who wrote the book, had no access to Zuckerberg or Facebook, though he did get some Facebook employees to talk to him on an anonymous basis. Given that Zuckerberg's friends and colleagues say he's attentive, funny, engaging, and a great guy, we are left with conflicting portraits. Who is the real Mark Zuckerberg?

Journalists who have interviewed him have, more often than not, left impressed. Even though he admits he doesn't care for the interviewing process, he can come across with considerable charm and likeability when he wants to—specifically, when he seems to feel the questions are interesting. But when the questions are banal, or exhibit cluelessness, he smiles knowingly, fires up his high-powered IQ, and uses a rapier-like wit to skewer the unwitting victim, who, caught off guard, cannot riposte.

Hacking is a revered word at Facebook. As *USA Today*'s Barbara Ortutay explained in a profile updated February 4, 2012, "It's an ideal that permeates the company's culture. It explains the push to try new ideas (even if they fail), and to promote new products quickly (even if they're imperfect). The hacker approach has made Facebook one of the world's most valuable Internet companies."

My interpretation is that, in short, Mark Zuckerberg doesn't suffer fools; he's simply dismissive and ignores them, and he shifts his attention elsewhere.

In this section we see the personal, not professional, side of the boy turned king.

***

Being Robbed

Explaining his brief encounter with a gun-toting thief who tried to rob him while he was filling up his gas tank at a service station: I'm just lucky to be alive. He didn't say what he wanted. I figured he was on drugs.

—Fast Company, *May 1, 2007*

Eliminating Desire

I just want to focus on what we're doing. When I put it in my profile, that's what I was focused on. I think it's probably Buddhist? To me it's just—I don't know, I think it would be very easy to get distracted and get caught up in short-term things or material things that don't matter. The phrase is actually, "Eliminating desire for all that doesn't really matter."

—Time, *December 27, 2010/January 3, 2011*

Advice to Students: Get With the Program

All of my friends who have younger siblings who are going to college or high school—my number one piece of advice is: You should learn how to program.

—Charlie Rose, *November 7, 2011*

Google+ Profile

I make things.

—Time: *Techland, July 5, 2011*

Getting Zucked

When interviewer Leslie Stahl falls back on discussing the world of celebrity, by saying, "You seem to be replacing [Google cofounders] Larry and Sergey as the people out there who everyone's talking about." Zuckerberg sniffed, paused, and blinked. "You're just staring at me," Stahl said. Zuckerberg responded: Is that a question?

—60 Minutes, *January 13, 2008*

Death Sentence

A Facebook user posted a contest called "Draw Mohammed Day" and incurred the wrath of the Muslim world, which held Zuckerberg responsible. His response: Someone is trying to get me sentenced to death in Pakistan now. That's not a joke. It might be funny, but it's not a joke. We think that what we're doing [at Facebook] is a really valuable thing in the world, and I hope I don't get killed.

—*Computer History Museum, July 21, 2010*

• •

Speaking Mandarin

Last year . . . my personal challenge was to learn Chinese. I blocked out an hour every day to study and it has been an amazing experience so far. I've always found learning new languages challenging, so I wanted to jump in and try to learn a hard one. It has been a very humbling experience. With language, there's no way to just "figure it out" like you can with other problems—you just need to practice and practice. The experience of learning Mandarin has also led me to travel to China, learn about its culture and history, and meet a lot of new interesting people.

—Fortune: *Postcards, May 26, 2011*

• •

Embracing *The Lord of the Flies*

I just killed a pig and a goat. [T]he only meat I'm eating is from animals I've killed myself. So far, this has been a good experience. . . . Every year I have a yearly personal challenge. It's a good way to explore different things I wouldn't normally do and challenge myself. Toward the end of last year I reflected a bunch on how thankful I was that we were building so many good things and things have gone well so far and I decided to make this year's challenge around being more thankful for what I have. I struggled for a while about how to implement this, but eventually decided that forcing myself to get personally involved and thank the animals whose lives I take in order to eat them was the best day-to-day way to remind myself to be thankful. So every day when I can't eat meat I am reminded of why not and how lucky I am, and when I do get the chance to eat meat it's especially good. The challenge also has the benefit of making me generally healthier, and I'm also learning a lot about sustainable living.

—*Comment on MZ's Facebook page, May 4, 2011, via* Fortune: *Postcards*

• •

Focus and Simplicity

In terms of doing work and in terms of learning and evolving as a person, you just grow more when you get more people's perspectives. ... I really try and live the mission of the company and . . . keep everything else in my life extremely simple.

—Charlie Rose, *November 7, 2011*

• •

Zuckerberg's Likes

On his personal Facebook page, Zuckerberg likes the following: openness, making things that help people connect and share what's important to them, revolutions, information flow, minimalism.

—*MZ's Facebook page, via* Business Insider

COLLEGE

Bill Gates gave Harvard's 2007 commencement address. When he discovered that the student newspaper had dubbed him *Harvard's most successful dropout*, he said, "I guess that makes me valedictorian of my own special class . . . I did the best of everyone who failed."

All joking aside, Gates spoke fondly of his time there.

> *Harvard was just a phenomenal experience for me. Academic life was fascinating. I used to sit in on lots of classes I hadn't even signed up for. And dorm life was terrific. I lived up at Radcliffe, in Currier House. There were always lots of people in my dorm room late at night discussing things, because everyone I knew didn't worry about getting up in the morning. ... What I remember above all about Harvard was being in the middle of so much energy and intelligence. It could be exhilarating, intimidating, sometimes even discouraging, but always challenging. It was an amazing privilege—and though I left early, I was transformed by my years at Harvard, the friendships I made, and the ideas I worked on.*

When Gates finally returned to Harvard to get his diploma, an honorary doctorate, he remarked, "I've been waiting more than 30 years to say this: 'Dad, I always told you I'd come back and get my degree.'... I'll be changing my job next year ... and it will be nice to finally have a college degree on my résumé."

The other famous Harvard dropout is, of course, Mark Zuckerberg, who took to heart what Gates said in his commencement address about the Internet: "The magical thing about this network is not just that it collapses distance and makes everyone your neighbor. It also dramatically increases the number of brilliant minds we can have working together on the same problem—and that scales up the rate of innovation to a staggering degree."

Beyond dropping out of Harvard, Zuckerberg, who as a sophomore attended a talk Bill Gates gave there, shares much in common with his fellow tech innovator: They're both exceptionally bright, curious, and they see technology as a game-changer. They both consider social networking as key to changing the world for the better.

What's important is not that Zuckerberg posted an irreverent website in college, or even that he dropped out after two years. What's important is that when he finally put the toys away, so to speak, he got down to the nitty-gritty: constructing Thefacebook, which commanded his attention to such an extent that he single-mindedly focused on it and persevered until it was ready for prime time. No discussion of Zuckerberg's college days would be complete without a mention of the Winklevoss twins, who recruited him to work on their Harvard dating website, HarvardConnection. There is no question that they asked him to work on the site, just as there is no question that Zuckerberg quickly abandoned it and went on to another project that he felt showed more promise—Thefacebook.

Given that the lawsuit that ensued is now history—Facebook settled for a reported $65 million in cash and stock—it seems moot to conduct a detailed postmortem. But it's worth pointing out that an idea is like a mental seed, and its successful germination depends entirely on the vision, imagination, and persistence of the mind into which it is planted.

***

. . . .

Mindset

Well I don't know business stuff. ... I'm content to
make something cool.

—*Instant messages to a friend, January 8, 2004, via*
Business Insider

. . . .

Animal Farm

*On his blog, Zuckerberg described his first online
foray into antisocial networking at Harvard, after
being dumped by his girlfriend:* [9:48 p.m.] I'm a
little intoxicated, not gonna lie. So what if it's not
even 10 p.m. and it's a Tuesday night? What? The
Kirkland [dormitory] facebook is open on my
desktop and some of these people have pretty hor-
rendous facebook pics. I almost want to put some
of these faces next to pictures of farm animals
and have people vote on which is more attractive.
[11:09 p.m.] Yea, it's on. I'm not exactly sure how
the farm animals are going to fit into this whole
thing (you can't really ever be sure with farm animals), but I like the idea of comparing two people
together. [12:58 a.m.] Let the hacking begin.

—*MZ's blog posts, February 4–5, 2004,
via* Huffington Post

••

No Job

My goal is not to have a job. Making cool things is just something I love doing, and not having someone tell me what to do or a timeframe in which to do it is the luxury I am looking for in my life. ... I assume eventually I'll make something that is profitable.

—Harvard Crimson, *June 10, 2004*

••

HarvardConnection

From emails sent to the HarvardConnection team, November 30, 2003: I read over all the stuff you sent and it seems like it shouldn't take too long to implement, so we can talk about that after I get all the basic functionality up tomorrow night. *December 1:* I put together one of the two registration pages so I have everything working on my system now. I'll keep you posted as I patch stuff up and it starts to become completely functional. *December 4:* Sorry I was unreachable tonight. I just got about three of your missed calls. I was working on a problem set. *December 10:* The week has been pretty busy thus far, so I haven't gotten a chance to do much work on the site or even think about it really, so I think

it's probably best to postpone meeting until we
have more to discuss. I'm also really busy tomorrow
so I don't think I'd be able to meet then anyway.
One week later: Sorry I have not been reachable
for the past few days. I've basically been in the lab
the whole time working on a cs [computer science]
problem set which I'm still not finished with.
January 8, 2004: Sorry it's taken a while for me
to get back to you. I'm completely swamped with
work this week. I have three programming projects and a final paper due by Monday, as well as a
couple of problem sets due Friday. I'll be available
to discuss the site again starting Tuesday.
I'm still a little skeptical that we have enough
functionality in the site to really draw the attention and gain the critical mass necessary to get a
site like this to run.

—*via* Business Insider

Hacking for the Fun of It

I do stuff like this all the time. The facebook liter-
ally took me a week to make. ... Half the things I
do I don't release. I spent five hours programming
last night, and came up with something that was
kind of cool, showed it to a bunch of my friends,
and the rest of the campus will never know about

it. ... I just like making it and knowing that it works and having it be wildly successful is cool, I guess, but I mean, I dunno, that's not the goal.

—Harvard Crimson, *June 10, 2004*

• •

Building Thefacebook

When I was getting started, with my roommates in college, you never think that you could build this company or anything like that, right? Because, I mean, we were college students, right? And we were just building stuff 'cause we thought it was cool. I do remember having these specific conversations with my friends where we thought, you know, someone is gonna build this. Someone is gonna build something that makes it so that people can stay connected with their friends and their family, but no way would we be the ones who were contributing to, kinda, leading the whole Internet in this direction.

—60 Minutes, *December 1, 2010*

• •

Zuckerberg's Initial Debt

We had a very simple focus and idea: The goal wasn't to make a huge community excited; it was to make something where you could type in someone's name and find out a bunch of information about them. . . . We ran the site originally for $85 a month, renting computers for the first three months. I was in debt $160, you know.

—Our Time, 2005, *via* Fast Company

Code Monkey

You know, in college, I just built a whole lot of different things. And that's just a passion of mine. It's, kind of, building things very quickly. . . . We [Zuckerberg and his early collaborators] figured, "Okay, this is something that may could grow to be a lot bigger." And that's . . . when my roommates joined me and we really started growing it aggressively.

—Business Insider, *October 14, 2010*

Backing Out of HarvardConnection

From an instant message to a friend describing Zuckerberg's work on HarvardConnection: I also hate the fact that I'm doing it for other people haha. Like I hate working under other people. I feel the right thing to do is finish the facebook and wait until the last day before I'm supposed to have their thing ready and then be like "look yours isn't as good as this so if you want to join mine you can . . . otherwise I can help you with yours later." Or do you think that's too dick?

> —*Instant message to Adam D'Angelo, fall 2002, via* Business Insider

• •

Psychology + CS = Facebook

In college I was a psychology major at the same time as being a computer science major. I say that fairly frequently, and people can't understand it. It's like, obviously I'm a CS person! But I was always interested in how those two things combined. For me, computers were always just a way to build good stuff, not like an end in itself.

> —Time, *December 27, 2010/January 3, 2011*

• •

Maturation

When I was in college I did a lot of stupid things, and I don't want to make an excuse for that. Some of the things that people accuse me of are true, some of them aren't. There are pranks, IMs. I started building [Facebook] when I was around 19 years old, and along the way, a lot of stuff changed.

We went from a building a service in a dorm room to running a service that 500 million people use.

—D8 Conference, 2010

....

Facebook's Origin

There are a few other things that I built when I was at Harvard that were kind of smaller versions of Facebook. One such program was this program called CourseMatch. People could enter the different courses that they were taking, and see what other courses would be correlated with the courses they are taking. And over my time at Harvard I built programs like that. On a small scale.

—Fast Company, September 17, 2009

....

Jettisoning Eduardo Saverin

I maintain that he fucked himself. ... He was supposed to set up the company, get funding, and make a business model. He failed at all three. ... Now that I'm not going back to Harvard I don't need to worry about getting beaten by Brazilian thugs. ... Eduardo is refusing to co-operate at all. ... We basically now need to sign over our intellectual property to a new company and just take the lawsuit. ... I'm just going to cut him out and then settle with him. And he'll get something I'm sure, but he deserves something. ... He has to sign stuff for investments and he's lagging and I can't take the lag.

—*Emails to Dustin Moskovitz and a third party, 2004,*
via Business Insider

●●●

Stock Dilution of Saverin's Shares

As far as Eduardo goes, I think it's safe to ask him to ask his permission to make grants. Especially if we do it in conjunction with raising money. It's probably even OK to say how many shares we're adding to the pool. It's probably less OK to tell him who's getting the shares, just because he might have [an] adverse reaction initially. But I think we may even be able to make him understand that. Is there a way to do this without making it painfully aware to him that he's being diluted to 10%?

—*Email to a lawyer, 2005 via* Business Insider

STARTING OUT

Silicon Valley is littered with the carcasses of dot-coms that went bust. Ineffective CEOs. Poor vision. Poor execution. Inadequate financing. Poor leadership. The list of startup sins is endless. As in any field, there's typically one company that rises to the top of the heap, and its success can be measured in terms of staying power and growth. And in the field of social networking, the undisputed number one company is Facebook.

As the saying goes, success has many parents but failure is an orphan. Who, after all, remembers MySpace? It had its day, but it's history in the fast-changing world of the web. Purchased by Rupert Murdoch's News Corporation in July 2005 for $580 million, it once had 1,600 employees, but it's now down to 200.[4] And in June 2011, it was sold at a staggering loss—the new buyers paid only $35 million, for 95 percent of the company.[5]

As Facebook's business model puts a premium on usefulness, MySpace probably lacked staying power because while cool, it was not useful.

Facebook had a shoestring budget when it was conceived. Even after Eduardo Saverin ponied up operating cash, the investment was modest. But what made the difference is Zuckerberg's vision. His interest in psychology proved useful, because it informed him that people are always most interested in other people. Whether in the real or virtual world, social networking is of paramount interest.

In this section, we see Zuckerberg's values and how they shaped Facebook's corporate culture. Those values and that culture go a long way toward explaining Facebook's worldwide appeal, dominant market share, and growing user base.

***

Silicon Valley's Culture

There's this culture in the Valley of starting a company before they know what they want to do. You decided you want to start a company, but you don't know what you are passionate about yet. ... You need to do stuff you are passionate about. The companies that work are the ones that people really care about and have a vision for the world, so do something you like.

—*Startup School, October 29, 2011*

Location, Location, Location

In response to the question, "What would be a better setting for new entrepreneurs today? Boston becoming more resourceful like Silicon Valley or Silicon Valley gaining the long term vision like you said?"
The point that I was trying to make wasn't that I couldn't have necessarily started Facebook in Boston or stayed here; it was that I think that there is more than one place where people can build companies. There's a feeling in Silicon Valley that you have to be there, because that's where all the engineers are. I just don't know if that's true. I think a lot of good companies get started all over the place. And often, I think a lot of people move out to Silicon Valley because that's where they have to

be, but there's so many smart people out here at MIT, Harvard, and other universities that you can start a company here, you can start a company in New York, you can start it in any country you want. That's basically the point I was trying to make.

—Remarks at MIT, November 8, 2011

• •

Silicon Valley's Short-Term Vision

There are aspects of the culture out here where I think it still is a little bit short-term focused in a way that bothers me. ... I think there's this culture out here where people don't commit to doing things. And there's nothing wrong with experimentations here—you need to do that before you dive in and decide that you're going to do something, but I feel like a lot of the companies that have built outside of Silicon Valley seem to be on a longer-term cadence than the ones in Silicon Valley for whatever reason.

—Startup School, October 29, 2011

• •

Dumb Mistakes

When asked about the "dumb things" he did when starting Facebook: Where do you want to start?

What kind of stuff do you want to start with? We weren't even set up as a company at first. I started it with different friends at Harvard who were really smart, and they didn't have the same levels of commitment. I moved to Silicon Valley, lots of folks didn't want to move out. A lot of the early founder group was fractured. I didn't want to be involved with setting up the business at all. We had this guy Eduardo. Instead of setting up a standard company, we set up as a Florida LLC. I don't know all the things wrong with that, but lawyers out here said that was number one to unwind. In the beginning we weren't trying to make it as big as possible. We wanted to provide value. Instead of launching schools that would be most receptive, we did least receptive. We launched at Stanford, Columbia, Yale, where each of them had their own community already. When we launched Facebook at those schools and it took off, we realized it could be worth putting our time into it. My friends are people who like building cool stuff. We always have this joke about people who want to just start companies without making something valuable. There's a lot of that in Silicon Valley. We wanted to be valuable.

—*Startup School, October 29, 2011*

●●●

MySpace and Facebook: Cool vs. Useful

When we got started, everyone compared us to MySpace. The big difference that we saw between ourselves and MySpace was that people used MySpace because it was cool and because it was fun. People ask us this question all the time: What's going to happen when Facebook is no longer cool? My answer to that question is that our goal is never to build something cool; it's to build something *useful*. Something that's cool is not going to be around for a long time. Something that's useful is around for a very long time potentially, if it continues to be useful. So when I say "utility," that's what I mean: We're trying to provide people with utility, not have something that's fun.

—Computer History Museum, July 21, 2010

FACEBOOK

Mission-Oriented

I think the biggest difference between Facebook
and other companies is how focused we are on our
mission. ... Different companies care about different things. There are companies that care about,
just really care about having the biggest market
cap. Or there are companies that are really into
process or the way they do things. Hewlett Packard,
right? The thing that you always hear about them
is "the HP Way." Google, I think is very tied to
their culture—they really love that. For us, it is the
mission: building a company that makes the world
more open and connected. The articulation of that
has, I think, changed over time. But that's really
been, like, the belief the whole time.

—Huffington Post, *May 14, 2012*

Independence

As a company we're very focused on what we're
building and not as focused on the exit. We just

believe that we're adding a certain amount of value to people's lives if we build a very good product. That's the reason why more than half of our users use the product every day—it's a more efficient way for them to communicate with their friends and get information about the people around them than anything else they can do. We're not really looking to sell the company. We're not looking to IPO anytime soon. It's just not the core focus of the company.

—Time, *July 17, 2007*

∙∙

Corporate Culture

If our mission is to make the world more open and connected, I certainly think that starts with us ourselves. We have this very open culture at the company. Every Friday afternoon, I get up and do a Q&A where anyone in the company can get up and ask me anything they want. One of the things I'm taking away from this is that if we want to lead the world and be the best service for this kind of sharing, that we should really probably be doing a lot more of it ourselves. I wouldn't characterize it as being a pitchman; I couldn't do that if I wanted to. But more open communication is good.

—Time, *May 27, 2010*

••

Board, Not Bored, Meetings

Well, Facebook is all about focus and not a lot of bureaucracy, so when we first started having our board meetings a few years back what I'd do is just start writing down a summary of what was going on with the business on a yellow piece of paper and give it to the board, and we used to have these really focused, great discussions of what was going on. Since then the board meetings have gotten a bit more structured: there's a bit more information handed out. But at the end of all the meetings our directors just say, "You know, I still love that single piece of paper with a summary of what's going on."

—Fast Company: *30 Second MBA*

••

Core Desire

I think that people just have this core desire to express who they are. And I think that's always existed.

—Charlie Rose, *November 7, 2011*

∙∙∙

Core Principles

- You have control over how your information is shared.
- We do not share your personal information with people or services you don't want.
- We do not give advertisers access to your personal information.
- We do not and never will sell any of your information to anyone.
- We will always keep Facebook a free service for everyone.

—Washington Post, *May 24, 2010*

∙∙∙

Reach

It's really the people themselves who have gotten us to this state. I mean, we've built a lot of products that we think are good and will help people share photos and share videos and write messages to each other. But it's really all about how people are spreading Facebook around the world in all these different countries. And that's what's so amazing about the scale that it's at today.

—ABC World News, *July 21, 2010*

••

Education

In 2010, Zuckerberg donated $100 million to a foundation to benefit Newark, New Jersey, schools: There are many different challenges all facing education at once. Teaching needs to be more respected and revered as a career. School districts need more autonomy and clearer leadership so they can be managed more like startups than like government bureaucracies. And outside the classroom, we need to support students' interests, give them a safe environment to grow up in, and keep everyone healthy.

—*Startup: Education, Facebook, September 24, 2010*

••

Goals

That's just like not something we're really interested in. I mean, yeah, we can make a bunch of money—that's not the goal . . . I mean, like, anyone from Harvard can get a job and make a bunch of money. Not everyone at Harvard can have a social network. I value that more as a resource more than, like, any money.

—Harvard Crimson, *June 10, 2004*

• •

Instagram

This is an important milestone for Facebook because it's the first time we've ever acquired a product and company with so many users. We don't plan on doing many more of these, if any at all. But providing the best photo sharing experience is one reason why so many people love Facebook and we knew it would be worth bringing these two companies together.

—*Facebook press release, April 9, 2012*

• •

Lawyers

Zuckerberg's line to leaders whose companies he's interested in acquiring: We don't need to get any lawyers involved. Let's just talk alone.

—New York Times, *May 12, 2012*

• •

Mobile Platforms

Mobile is a huge opportunity for Facebook. Our goal is to connect everyone in the world. And over the next 5 years, we expect 4 billion to 5 billion people to have smartphones. That's more than twice as many people that have computers today.

So building great services for these devices is essential for us to help people connect. We also think that people are inherently social, and having a device with you wherever you are creates more opportunities for sharing and connecting.

—*Seeking Alpha, July 26, 2012*

News Feed

On its controversial feature, News Feed, when a user termed it "just too creepy, too stalker-esque, and a feature that has to go."
We agree, stalking isn't cool; but being able to know what's going on in your friends' lives is. This is information people used to dig for on a daily basis, nicely reorganized and summarized so people can learn about the people they care about. None of your information is visible to anyone who couldn't see it before the changes.

—*Facebook Blog, September 5, 2006*

In Touch

Until recently, there hasn't been a good system for you to keep in touch with all of the other people who are in your life who you meet at some point

who are important or were important and you
want to keep up with, but you don't have a way to
talk to on a day to day basis, and you wouldn't go
out of your way to call, and you would never sit
down with them in person. It's the power that's
unlocked from that is what we're seeing here.
When you can build up the value of all of those
latent connections and keep them open, this is the
type of stuff that becomes possible. But it's because
they want to do it on their own anyway; we're just
allowing people the ability to do those things.

—*Computer History Museum, July 21, 2010*

. . . .

Online Directory

[Facebook is] essentially an online directory for
students. Where people can go and look up other
people and find relevant information about them.
Everything from what they're interested in, to
their contact information, what courses they're
taking, who they know, who their friends are,
what people say about them, what photos they
have now. I guess it's mostly utility for people to
figure out just what's going on in their lives and in
their friends' lives for people they care about.

—*Entrepreneurial Thought Leaders Seminars,*
Stanford, 2005

. . . .

Openness

So, I guess, like, by doing this we kind of created a culture where people just talk to each other about stuff, and get what each other is thinking more clearly than they would if the organization was more bureaucratic. Or, if like people wouldn't be heard. And then I mean, since people are always talking, ideas get bounced off each other and then eventually, like, someone starts making something, you know, and then we're done.

—*Entrepreneurial Thought Leaders Seminars, Stanford, 2005*

. . . .

People-Centric

From the beginning, Facebook hasn't been about building a website. Facebook is about all of the people using it and all of the things that are important to you.

—*Facebook Blog, July 15, 2009*

. . . .

Connecting

Whether in times of tragedy or joy, people want to share and help one another. This human need is what inspires us to continue to innovate and build things that allow people to connect easily and share their lives with one another.

—Facebook Blog, February 4, 2010

● ●

Information Control

Our philosophy is that people own their information and control who they share it with. When a person shares information on Facebook, they first need to grant Facebook a license to use that information so that we can show it to other people they've asked us to share it with. Without this license, we couldn't help people share that information.

—Facebook Blog, February 16, 2009

● ●

Sharing

Film producer/director Barry Sonnenfeld asked Zuckerberg if, based on the experience of Sonnenfeld's 15-year-old daughter who "has no sense of privacy," the company is "creating a generation where there's no fear of government, no fear of loss of privacy."

Share, share, share. Share, share, share. You can set up filters, settings so you can figure out who you want to share, share, share your information with. And even though it seems like [your] daughter doesn't care, a huge amount of our users are tweaking their settings. So they're aware of it.

—*D6 Conference, 2008*

••

Privacy

Six years ago, we built Facebook around a few simple ideas. People want to share and stay connected with their friends and the people around them. If we give people control over what they share, they will want to share more. If people share more, the world will become more open and connected. And a world that's more open and connected is a better world. These are still our core principles today.

—Washington Post, *May 24, 2010*

••

Privacy Settings

The challenge is how a network like ours facilitates sharing and innovation, offers control and choice, and makes this experience easy for everyone. These are issues we think about all the time. Whenever we make a change, we try to apply the lessons we've learned along the way. The biggest message we have heard recently is that people want easier control over their information. Simply put, many of you thought our controls were too complex. Our intention was to give you lots of granular controls; but that may not have been what many of you wanted. We just missed the mark.

—Washington Post, *May 24, 2010*

. . . .

Privacy Tools

The real question for me is, do people have the tools that they need in order to make those decisions well? And I think that it's actually really important that Facebook continually makes it easier and easier to make those decisions. ... If people feel like they don't have control over how they're sharing things, then we're failing them.

—Charlie Rose, *November 7, 2011*

. . . .

Privacy from Day One

I founded Facebook on the idea that people want to share and connect with people in their lives, but to do this everyone needs complete control over who they share with at all times.
This idea has been the core of Facebook since day

one. When I built the first version of Facebook, almost nobody I knew wanted a public page on the Internet. That seemed scary. But as long as they could make their page private, they felt safe sharing with their friends online. Control was key. With Facebook, for the first time, people had the tools they needed to do this. That's how Facebook became the world's biggest community online. We made it easy for people to feel comfortable sharing things about their real lives.

—*Facebook Blog, November 29, 2011*

••

Sharing Information

I think that these companies with those big ad networks are basically getting away with collecting huge amounts of information. … But I think because people can see how much information people are sharing about themselves on Facebook, it appears scarier.

—Charlie Rose, *November 7, 2011*

· ·

Self-Revelations

The question isn't "What do we want to know about people?" It's "What do people want to tell about themselves?"

—Charlie Rose, *November 7, 2011*

· ·

Information Conduit

Creating channels between people who want to work together towards change has always been one of the ways that social movements push the world forward and make it better. Both U.S. President Barack Obama and French President Nicholas Sarkozy have used Facebook as a way to organize their supporters. From the protests against the Columbian FARC, a 40-year-old terrorist organization, to fighting oppressive, fringe groups in India, people use Facebook as a platform to build connections and organize action.

—*Facebook Blog, April 8, 2009*

· ·

Virtual Friends, Virtually Forever

Facebook wants to . . . turn the lonely, antisocial world of random chance into a friendly world, a serendipitous world. You'll be working and living inside a network of people, and you'll never have to be alone again. The Internet, and the whole world, will feel more like a family, or a college dorm, or an office where your co-workers are also your best friends.

—Time, *December 27, 2010/January 3, 2011*

• •

The Super Power of Word of Mouth

I think the basic idea here is that there is a phenomenon in people's interaction. The message that you get, in a lot of ways, is actually less important than who you get it from. It you get it from someone that you trust a lot more, then you really listen to it, whereas if you get it from someone you don't trust, you might actually believe the opposite of what they said because you don't trust them. I think that's the basis of value that people get on the site. I go to someone's profile and see that they like this band. That means more to me than if I just saw a billboard for that band. We figured that in the really organic way to make money and sustain the company, that these interests would be aligned.

—Fast Company, *September 17, 2009*

LAWSUITS

With success comes litigation.

As soon as Zuckerberg went live, Thefacebook drew the attention, and the ire, of the Winklevoss twins and Divya Narendra, who wanted their recompense—with interest—from Zuckerberg, whom they claimed had committed IP theft. Harvard-Connection, they said, was the original idea for Facebook.

Following the Winklevoss/Narendra lawsuit, a lawsuit was filed by Paul Ceglia, who claimed half ownership of Facebook, based on a contract he had with Zuckerberg. In a March 26, 2012, article for CNNMoney, Julianne Pepitone explains, "Ceglia claims the contract also covered work on a fledgling site called 'the Face Book,' something Zuckerberg strenuously disputes. The timelines don't match up: Ceglia's alleged contract is dated several months before Zuckerberg began working on the project that became Facebook."

Orin Snyder, an attorney retained by Facebook, filed a dismissal motion alleging, "Ceglia has forged documents, destroyed evidence, and abused the judicial system in furtherance of his criminal scheme. Ceglia must be held accountable."[6]

What is yet to come: the "unwieldy mass of legal claims" (numbering more than 40) in the wake of Facebook's botched IPO. According to the *New York Times* ("Dealing With the Facebook Law-suits," by Peter J. Henning and Steven M. Davidoff, June 18, 2012), Facebook asserts that NASDAQ is at fault for its opening day glitches. The result: Face-book and the investors in question will have their day in court.

***

··

Every Capitalist

On the HarvardConnection team: Instead, from these conversations, it became apparent that [they] were not as clued-in and business-savvy as they had led me to believe. It almost seemed like my most socially inept friends at the school had a better idea of what would attract people to a website than these guys. ... After that meeting I began making thefacebook, and I did not hear from them until about one week ago when I received their demand letters, threatening to bring me before the [Harvard] ad board on ethical grounds.

As a bit of background, I try not to get involved with other students' ventures since they are generally too time-consuming and don't provide me with enough room to be creative and do my own thing. Frankly, I'm kind of appalled that they're threatening me after the work I've done for them free of charge, but after dealing with a bunch of other groups with deep pockets and good legal connections including companies like Microsoft, I can't say I'm surprised. I try to shrug it off as a minor annoyance that whenever I do something successful, every capitalist out there wants a piece of the action.

—*Email to Harvard dean John Walsh,*
February 17, 2004

••

I Fought the Law and the Law Won

On the Winklevoss brothers' out-of-court settle-ment worth a reported $65 million and their fur-ther claim that they were ripped off: You know, it's hard for me to fully wrap my head around where they're coming from on this. You know, early on, they had an idea that was completely separate from Facebook. And that, I mean, it was a dating site for Harvard. And I agreed to help them out with it, to help them. Right, I mean, it wasn't a job, they weren't paying me, I wasn't hired by them or anything like that. And then, the idea that I would then go work on something completely different, like Facebook, and that they would be upset about this all these years later is kinda mindboggling for me. Now, I mean, this is another thing that I think the movie [*The Social Network*] really missed is, I mean, they make it seem like this whole lawsuit is such a huge part of Facebook's history. I've probably spent less than two weeks of my time worried about this lawsuit at all, right? . . . I mean, after all this time, I feel bad that they still feel bad about it.

—60 Minutes, *December 1, 2010*

• •

Big Brother Is Watching

In response to ongoing privacy concerns, the Federal Trade Commission (FTC) released an agreement with Facebook that included the following: "The proposed settlement bars Facebook from making any further deceptive privacy claims, requires that the company get consumers' approval before it changes the way it shares their data, and requires that it obtain periodic assessments of its privacy practices by independent, third-party auditors for the next 30 years."

Zuckerberg's blog post on the issue: Even before the agreement announcement by the FTC today, Facebook has already proactively addressed many of the concerns the FTC raised. For example, their complaint to us mentioned our Verified Apps Program, which we canceled almost two years ago in December 2009. The same complaint also mentions cases where advertisers inadvertently received the ID numbers of some users in referrer URLs. We fixed that problem over a year ago in May 2010.

In addition to these product changes, the FTC also recommended improvements to our internal processes. We've embraced these ideas, too, by agreeing to improve and formalize the way we do privacy review as part of our ongoing product development process. As part of this, we will establish a biannual independent audit of our privacy practices to ensure we're living up to the commitments we make.

—Facebook Blog, November 29, 2011.

THE SOCIAL NETWORK

Hollywood didn't set out to create an honest documentary of Facebook; scenes of hackers writing strings of computer code won't fill the seats at your local cinema. A highly dramatized biography of the company, however, is an obvious money-maker.

In the case of *The Social Network*—based on Ben Mezrich's book *The Accidental Billionaires: The Founding of Facebook*—the result was a skewed portrait of Zuckerberg and Facebook.

Mezrich writes in an author's note, "I do employ the technique of re-created dialogue. I have based this dialogue on the recollections of participants of the substance of conversations."

So what you are getting with his book, and the movie adaptation based on it, is a highly interpretive, imperfect version of Facebook's history.

***

••

The Social Network

It's a movie. It's fun. A lot of it is fiction, but even the filmmakers will say that. They're trying to build a good story. This is my life so I know it's not that dramatic. … Maybe it would be fun to remember it as partying and all this crazy drama but who knows? Maybe it'll be an interesting story.

—ABC News, *September 24, 2010*

••

The Social Network's Depiction of Zuckerberg

Where do you want to start? The thing that I think is actually most thematically interesting that they got wrong is the whole framing of the movie. They frame it as if the whole reason for making Facebook and building something was because I wanted to get girls. They just can't wrap their head around the idea that some-one might build something because they like building things.

—Moviefone, *October 19, 2010*

●●

The Social Network's Positive Aspects

And I can't tell you how many messages I've gotten from people who use Facebook writing in to say, "This movie was really inspiring to me. After seeing this movie, I want to start a company." Or "I want to go into computer science," or "I want to study math." And if the movie had that affect on people, then awesome, right? I mean, that's great.

—60 Minutes, *December 1, 2010*

MISSION

It all boils down to this: What is the mission? From the beginning, Facebook's mission has evolved, but never changed. Gillian Reagan analyzed Facebook's mission statements from 2004 to 2009 in "The Evolution of Facebook's Mission Statement," which ran in the *New York Observer* on July 12, 2009.[7] Here are the statements she looked at, along with the most current mission for the company, for you to judge for yourself.

- 2004: Thefacebook is an online directory that connects people through social networks at colleges.
- 2007: Facebook is a social utility that connects you with the people around you.
- 2008: Facebook helps you connect and share with the people in your life.
- 2009: Facebook gives people the power to share and make the world more open and connected.
- 2012: Facebook's mission is to give people the power to share and make the world more open and connected.

***

• •

Ubiquity

Our goal is not to build a platform—it's to be across all of them.

—Charlie Rose, *November 7, 2011*

• •

Long-Range Vision

I'm here to build something for the long term. Anything else is a distraction.

—Fast Company, *May 1, 2007*

• •

Steve Jobs

He was amazing. I had a lot of questions for him
on . . . how to build a team around you that's
focused on building as high quality and good
things as you are. How to keep an organization
focused, when I think the tendency for larger
companies is to try to fray and go into all these
different areas. Yeah, I mean a lot just on the
aesthetics and kind of mission orientation of
companies. Apple is a company that is so focused
on just building products that—for their customers and their users—it's such a deep part of their
mission [to] build these beautiful products for
their users. And I think we connected a lot on this
level.

Facebook has this mission that's really more than
just trying to build a company that has a market
cap or a value. It's like we're trying to do this thing
in the world. I just think we connected on that
level.

—Charlie Rose, *November 7, 2011*

PROCESS

Facebook has its own version of the Force—that secret glue that holds the *Star Wars* universe together. As Obi-Wan Kenobi explains, the Force is "an energy field created by all living things. It surrounds us, penetrates us, and binds the galaxy together."

In the Facebook universe, the Force is called *hacking*.

***

Product Improvement

Comparing the iterative nature of computer coding to journalism: It's iterative, right? You'll write it, then next year you'll write another story, and another, and eventually, the story will be the way you want it.

—Fast Company, *March 19, 2012*

● ●

On Innovation

A lot of people think that innovation is just having your great idea. But a lot of it is just moving quickly and trying a lot of things. So at Facebook we've really built our whole company and our whole culture around that. We do things like shift code every single day. And we have this tradition of having hackathons which are events where all of our engineers, and really the whole company, get together and stay up just all night building things, whatever they want, not just what they're doing for work, just trying things out and innovating.

—Fast Company: *30 Second MBA*

● ●

On Focus

Our job is to stay focused on building the best service for [third-party social applications]. And if we do that, then there's a massive market and a lot of value to be built in the world. And if we don't, then someone else will do it.

—Fast Company, *July 6, 2011*

• •

Social Context and Serendipity

We have this concept of serendipity—humans do. A lucky coincidence. ... When you have this kind of context of what's going on, it's just going to make people's lives richer, because instead of missing 99% of them, maybe now you'll start seeing a lot more of them.

—Time, *December 27, 2010/January 3, 2011*

• •

First Things First

I think a simple rule of business is, if you do the things that are easier first, then you can actually make a lot of progress.

—Charlie Rose, *November 7, 2011*

• •

Fast Movers

The whole company is really optimized around someone joining, being able to build something very quickly, be able to launch it quickly, iterate very quickly on that. Get feedback quickly. That

moving fast ethos is a huge part of what we do
.... And we have this belief that you never build
something great by doing the same way that other
people have done it. ... For the core things that we
wanna do, when we have the decision to either do
it the same way that someone else has done it or
do it a different way, we're gonna choose to do it
in a different way. And we really encourage people
all throughout the company to think about things
in that way and make bolder decisions.

—Business Insider, *October 14, 2010*

The Hacker's Way

Can we take what used to take 10 clicks for someone to get the information they need and reduce
it to three? It saves time over thousands of opera-
tions. What can we do with that time?

—Fast Company, *March 19, 2012*

Hacking's Good

When we say "hacker," there's this whole defini-
tion that engineers have for themselves where it's
very much a compliment when you call someone
a hacker, where to hack something means to build

something very quickly, right? In one night, you can sit down and you can churn out a lot of code, and at the end, you have a product.

—60 Minutes, *December 1, 2010*

• •

Hackathons

We want to make sure that everyone can come and add their ideas. I mean, some of the best ideas throughout the company's evolution, they have just been from just places all throughout the company, whether it's an engineer or someone on the customer support team or just different areas around the company. So we've always had these hackathons that are basically time that we allocate that, the only rule is that you don't work on what you work on the rest of the time. It's basically an incubator for people to prototype different ideas, much in the spirit of how Facebook got founded originally. You can build anything good in a day, or a couple of days . . . and get a version of that running.

—Business Insider, *October 14, 2010*

VALUES

· ·

No Games

On why Zuckerberg believes Facebook won't get into game development: What we're doing is really hard. And we think that we're better off focusing on this piece [building social networks]. I think that building a great game service is really hard. Building a great music service is really hard. Building a great movie service is really hard. And we just believe that an independent entrepreneur will always beat a division of a big company which is why we think that the strategy of these other companies trying to do everything themselves will inevitably be less successful than an ecosystem where you have someone like Facebook trying to build the core product to help people connect and then independent great companies that are only focused on one or two things doing those things really well.

—Charlie Rose, *November 7, 2011*

••

Making Mistakes

So many businesses get worried about looking like they might make a mistake, they become afraid to take any risk. Companies are set up so that people judge each other on failure. I'm not going to get fired if we have a bad year. Or a bad five years. I don't have to worry about making things look good if they're not. I can actually set up the company to create value.

—Fast Company, *March 19, 2012*

••

Getting Things Done

There's an intense focus on openness, sharing information, as both an ideal and a practical strategy to get things done.

—Fast Company, *May 1, 2007*

••

Siding with the Underdog

Explaining why Facebook chose to partner with Bing rather than Google: They [Microsoft] really are the underdog here. They're incentivized to go out and innovate. When you're an incumbent in an area . . . there is tension between innovating and trying new things versus what you already have.

—Fast Company, *October 14, 2010*

....

Caring

I guess what it probably turns out is, other people didn't care as much as we did.

—Time, *December 27, 2010/January 3, 2011*

....

Users' Privacy Controls

The way that people think about privacy is changing a bit. What people want isn't complete privacy. It isn't that they want secrecy. It's that they want control over what they share and what they don't.

—Time, *May 20, 2010*

....

Entrepreneur/CEO

On the qualities that make good entrepreneurs and CEOs: One is just having a really strong sense of what you want to do, because along the way there are so many distractions that if you're not completely clear on what you want to do, you're going to get sidetracked. That's number one: being clear about what you want to do, and really caring about it.

Number two is building a good team. That's what I spend a huge amount of time on. When I'm not building products—I work with teams to build products—so it goes all the way down the organization from really good head of engineering and getting the best hackers and engineers and people who want to build stuff, to the head of product who can really communicate exactly what you're going to do, and make sure that every person in the company knows what the plan is, to really good business folks like Sheryl [Sandberg]. . . .

Should I run the company or not? If I were to disappear, any of them could run the company. If you have a clear idea of what you're doing and you have great people, then that's a lot of the battle.

—*Computer History Museum, July 21, 2010*

••

Not Selling Out

So we had this episode where Yahoo and Viacom and all these companies were trying to buy the company. And it was this really kind of crazy time. Because we started the company as a dorm room project. Actually we started it specifically *not* as a company, just a project, and we had this whole conversation about whether we wanted to turn it into a company or a partnership or what, and we ended up deciding a company was the best way to go because that's the best way you can attract really good people and incentivize them to build something great.

We reached a point where, you know, me and my friends, we were 22 years old, people were offering us a billion dollars or more for the company, and it's like—what do you do? Right? So we didn't want to sell the company. Obviously we didn't sell the company.

But it was really pivotal point for us, because when you're 22 and have an opportunity to sell something for that much money, you reach this point where, like, you're not making decisions to maximize the amount of money that you're making. Where I mean, like, any amount of money would not be worth the, like, the last few years that we've spent building up the company.

—Press conference, May 28, 2010

••

Employees' Leverage

We've always been significantly smaller per employee compared to the number of people who we serve in the world. So it's really baked into the company that we have to build systems and software that take into account the leverage that employees here have. And that's actually one of the reasons why a lot of people love working here and one of the biggest reasons why people cite for wanting to join the company and staying here. So it's also affected the strategy. I mentioned we believe that all these consumer products, and maybe even more than consumer products that people use, will become social over time.

—*Seeking Alpha, July 26, 2012*

••

The Power of Focus

I've always focused on a couple of things. ... One is having a clear direction for the company and what we build. And the other is just trying to build the best team possible toward that. ... I think, as a company, if you can just get those two things right—having a clear direction on what you are trying to do, and bringing in great people who can execute on the stuff—then you can do pretty well.

—*D8 Conference, 2010*

••

Creating Value

I don't think of myself as a businessperson. I just think that one of the things that's amazing about the Internet is if you build something good that is a service that is valuable for people, it can spread quickly and if you create value for other people, then you might be able to realize a portion of that value yourself. I never thought about Facebook as starting a business that would grow its own value, but in a way I think it's really good that the world works this way. ... [I]f someone does something that's valuable that that's enough to build a good business. ... I don't think that I've focused on a lot of the same things that a lot of other business-people do, but every day we try to come in and build the best product for people.

—Time, *2010*

••

Employees Growing on the Job

We do try to attract people, but our goal isn't nec-essarily to keep people forever. Some companies are really good at training people. A lot of people for a long time went to IBM because it was great to learn sales. We want Facebook to be one of the best places people can go to learn how to build stuff. If you want to build a company, nothing's better than jumping in and trying to build one. But Facebook is also great for entrepreneurs/hackers. If people want to come for a few years and move on and build something great, that's something we're proud of. Steve Chen when he started working on YouTube was working on Facebook. They left, did something cool. I'm not encouraging people working at Facebook to leave. We're not pretending that we're building a company that hackers would want to stay at forever.

—*Startup School, October 29, 2011*

. . . .

Measuring Value

In response to interviewer Guy Raz's observation that Facebook "is worth $27 billion": I mean, who cares? I measure it in terms of the number of people who are working on it.

—*Computer History Museum, July 21, 2010*

••

Building Companies

Building a company is one of the most efficient ways in the world that you can kind of align the incentives of a lot of smart people towards making a change.

—*Startup School, October 29, 2011*

••

Facebook's Biggest Challenges

The two things that you focus on are maintaining what you have now that's good and growing. … Focusing on things that are sustainable and skillable, and so that when we launched more skills, or go on to the next market, we are going to set ourselves up to have the same success we've had without hurting ourselves in the current position. It's basically maintaining the utility while growing.

—*Entrepreneurial Thought Leaders Seminars,*
Stanford, 2005

••

Prioritizing

The most important thing that we should be doing
as a business is prioritizing, figuring out what the
right things are for us to be approaching now. ...
[W]orking on stuff that's really important now is
always like the best use of our time.

—Entrepreneurial Thought Leaders Seminars,
Stanford, 2005

••

Hiring Employees

The two most important things that I look for are,
number one, raw intelligence; I think that that's
the most important thing that I look for. And the
second: just alignment with what we're trying to
do. People can be really smart, or have skills that
are directly applicable, but if they don't really
believe in it, then they are not going to really work
hard.

—Entrepreneurial Thought Leaders Seminars,
Stanford, 2005

● ●

Motivation

The demands and the amount of work it takes to put something like [Facebook] into place, it's just so much that if you weren't completely into what you were doing and you didn't think it was an important thing, then it would be irrational to spend that much time on it. ... People constantly try to put us in a bucket: are we trying to sell the company? What are we trying to do? What is the business strategy? . . . Whereas for me and a lot of people around me, that's not really what we focus on. We're just focused on building things.

—Time, *July 17, 2007*

● ●

The Next Big Thing

I don't really know what the next big thing is because I don't spend my time making big things. I spend time making small things and then when the time comes I put them together.

—Harvard Crimson, *June 10, 2004*

••

Fast and Faster

We can always be innovating more, doing more things. ... I'm just an impatient person, right. I want to see us, like, release all these products very quickly, and—and that's like—that's a big thing for—for our company. We love moving fast, and being bold, and kind of making those big things.

—ABC World News, *July 21, 2010*

••

Selling Out

On Yahoo's 2006 bid for Facebook, which dropped from $1 billion to $850 million after its own stock took a precipitous drop: If you don't want to sell your company, don't get into a process where you're talking to people about selling your company.

—New York Times, *May 12, 2012*

ACCOUNTABILITY

When your modus operandi as a company is to move fast and break things, one thing constantly at risk of breaking is the connection with the users. The worst thing to do is ignore the complaints. The second worst thing is gloss over them and give a perfunctory explanation. Facebook found out the hard way when it committed both sins, alienating its user base that, naturally, went online to Facebook to air its dissatisfaction.

In *The Boy Kings*, author Katerine Losse writes that when Facebook launched News Feed, users were outraged and wrote Facebook to complain. Losse, a customer service rep at the time, sent a stock reply: "This information was already available to your friends on Facebook; we're just delivering it more efficiently."

Major fail.

Then, Facebook compounded the error. According to Losse: "With the click of a button, [customer service] blasted the stock News Feed response email to everyone who had written in that day, whether their query had to do with News Feed or not."

With the Facebook community at large in an uproar, Zuckerberg finally stepped in to resolve the matter.

Lesson learned: If you screw up, admit it right away, and then move on.

**

Stepping In It and Scraping It Off

We really messed this one up. When we launched News Feed and Mini-Feed we were trying to provide you with a stream of information about your social world. Instead, we did a bad job of explaining what the new features were and an even worse job of giving you control of them. I'd like to correct those errors now. ... This may sound silly, but I want to thank all of you who have written in and created groups and protested. Even though I wish I hadn't made so many of you angry, I am glad we got to hear you. And I am also glad that News Feed highlighted all these groups so people could find them and share their opinions with each other as well.

—*Facebook Blog, September 8, 2006*

On FTC Allegations of Privacy Violations

I'm the first to admit that we've made a bunch of mistakes.

—*Facebook Blog, November 29, 2011*

VISION

SOPA (Stop Online Piracy) and PIPA (Protect Intellectual Property Act)

The Internet is the most powerful tool we have for creating a more open and connected world. We can't let poorly thought out laws get in the way of the Internet's development. Facebook opposes SOPA and PIPA, and we will continue to oppose any laws that will hurt the Internet. The world today needs political leaders who are pro-Internet. We have been working with many of these folks for months on better alternatives to these current proposals. I encourage you to learn more about these issues and tell your congressmen that you want them to be pro-Internet.

—*Facebook Blog, January 18, 2012*

A Blinding Flash of the Obvious

Isn't it obvious that everyone was going to be on the Internet? Isn't it, like, inevitable that there would be a huge social network of people? It was something that we expected to happen. The thing that's been really surprising about the evolution of Facebook is—I think then and I think now—that if we didn't do this, someone else would have done it.

—New Yorker, *September 20, 2010*

· ·

On the Future of Email

We don't think that a modern messaging system is going to be email. It's not email. It's a messaging system that includes email as a part of it. This is not an email killer. We don't expect anyone to say, "I'm going to shut down my Yahoo or Gmail account and switch exclusively to Facebook." We don't think that's what's happening in the world. Whether it's one day in six months, or a year, or two years, this is the way the future should work.

—Fast Company, *October 14, 2010*

· ·

Risk-Taking

The biggest risk is not taking any risk. ... In the world that changes really quickly, the only strategy that is guaranteed to fail is not taking risks.

—*Startup School, October 29, 2011*

• •

Facebook's Future

We don't think we're anywhere near the end [of Facebook]. What we've seen is that there's this massive trend on the Internet towards there being all kinds of information available. Google came out when I was middle school. There were these search engines. Growing up, every year . . . there was some new, cool thing. There were all these different services. The thing I think that's most interesting to people is other people, so I think it makes sense in a way that Facebook is by far the most engaging app that's been built online to date.

—*Computer History Museum, July 21, 2010*

• •

Social Trending

I certainly think that the trend we're operating on now of helping people share information, which is really something that, going back twenty years ago, most people in society did not have the power to do; the Internet has really brought that about. Now everyone can share their opinions and information about themselves or what's going on around them, and that's a new thing. That's the trend we're hoping to push forward. That's going to be one of the most transformative trends in society over the next ten, fifteen [years], I mean, who knows how long?

—*Computer History Museum, July 21, 2010*

. . . .

The Evolution of Mass Communication Tools

We often talk about inventions like the printing press and the television—by simply making communication more efficient, they led to a complete transformation of many important parts of society. They gave more people a voice. They encouraged progress. They changed the way society was organized. They brought us closer together.

—Charlie Rose, *November 7, 2011*

. . . .

Responsible Governments

We expect governments will become more responsible to issues and concerns raised directly by all their people rather than through intermediaries controlled by a select few.

—Charlie Rose, *November 7, 2011*

••

A Social Web

We're building a web where the default is social.

—Time, *May 20, 2010*

••

Responsibilities

I think the CEO basically does two things: They set the vision for the company, and they recruit a team. So far, we have this vision and we're in the middle of executing it, and we're only four years done, so I think there's a lot left to go. And building a team is a really important piece of that. We spend a lot of time focused on that.

—*D6 Conference, 2008*

••

Information Sharing

I would expect that next year, people will share twice as much information as they share this year, and the next year, they will be sharing twice as much as they did the year before. That means that people are using Facebook, and the applications and the ecosystem, more and more.

—New York Times, *November 6, 2008*

• •

Companies Admired

Amazon is a great recent example of focusing on the long term and accepting shorter margins on the short term. Jeff [Bezos] went through years of people thinking he's crazy. Apple is amazing in terms of the quality of stuff that they do. And Google, too, for the same thing.

—Wall Street Journal, *January 14, 2012*

• •

Transparency in History

History tells us that systems are most fairly governed when there is an open and transparent dialogue between the people who make decisions and those who are affected by them. We believe history will one day show that this principle holds true for companies as well, and we're looking to moving in this direction with you.

—*Facebook Blog, February 26, 2009*

••

Monetizing: Cash In by Cashing Out

When asked by an audience member, "How do you best monetize as an exit strategy?"

I spend my time thinking about how to build this and not how to exit. I think that what we're doing is more interesting than what anyone else is doing . . . that this is just a cool thing to be doing. I don't spend time thinking about [an exit strategy] that much. Sorry.

—*Entrepreneurial Thought Leaders Seminars, Stanford, 2005*

••

The Web's Future

We think that the future of the web will be filled with personalized experiences. . . . For example, now if you're logged into Facebook and go to Pandora for the first time, it can immediately start playing songs from bands you've liked across the web. And as you're playing music, it can show you friends who also like the same songs as you, and then you can click to see other music they like.

—*Facebook Blog, April 21, 2010*

• •

On the Future of Social Networking

I think the next five years are going to be about building out this social platform. It's about the idea that most applications are going to become social, and most industries are going to be rethought in a way where social design and doing things with your friends is at the core of how these things work.

—Time, *December 27, 2010/January 3, 2011*

PHILANTHROPY

Early Philanthropy

A lot of people wait until later in their careers to think about how to give back, and I just had a bunch of conversations with my friends and people who I work with recently where it really occurred to me, "Why wait another 15 or 20 years when I'll have a lot more time to focus on it, but if we already have the resources we should probably get started on it now." Hopefully, participating in this encourages other people in our generation to do so as well.

—Time, *2010*

Organ Donations

Facebook is really about communicating and telling stories. ... We think that people can really help spread awareness of organ donation and that they want to participate in this to their friends. And that can be a big part of helping solve the crisis that's out there. ... We want to make it simple. You just put in the state or country that you're from, so that we can help link you to the official registries.

—ABC News, *May 1, 2012*

••

The Power of Friends

Facebook is about connecting and sharing—
connecting with your friends, family and communities, and sharing information with them about your
life, work, school, and interests. On any given day,
more than half a billion people share billions of stories, updates, and photos. What has amazed us over
the past eight years is how people use these same
tools and social dynamics to address important issues
and challenges in their communities. Last year in
Missouri, Facebook users tracked down and returned
treasured mementos to families who thought they'd
lost everything in the Joplin tornado. In Japan, people
used Facebook to locate family and friends following the 2011 earthquake and tsunami. Smaller acts of
kindness happen millions of times a day on Facebook.

We could never have anticipated that what started as a
small network would evolve into such a powerful tool
for communication and problem solving. As this hap-
pens, we hope to build tools that help people transform
the way we all solve worldwide social problems. . . .

But the Facebook community has also shown us
that simply through sharing and connecting, the
world gets smaller and better. Even one individual
can have an outsized impact on the challenges fac-
ing another, and on the world. At Facebook, we call
that the power of friends.

—ABC News, *May 2, 2012*

MARK ZUCKERBERG'S LETTER TO INVESTORS

When Zuckerberg was a sophomore at Harvard, the school newspaper, *The Harvard Crimson*, covered Facebook's birth and subsequent growth.

Since that time, media coverage of Zuckerberg has been extensive. Fans and detractors alike have weighed in, offering their perspectives on him and his company. Their collective views, predictably, vary wildly.

For those who want to glean insights on Facebook through the eyes of its principal figure, this letter illuminates Zuckerberg's thoughts.

Included in Facebook's Form S-1 Registration Statement and filed February 1, 2012, this letter has been subsequently republished numerous times on the Internet. In it, Zuckerberg speaks plainly and to the point—and for good reason: It is his voice, his insights, and his vision that prospective investors are interested in. In short, it's a letter that buttresses the IPO.

As others have pointed out online, Zuckerberg's letter is required reading for anyone interested in Facebook—especially investors.

Letter from Mark Zuckerberg

Facebook was not originally created to be a company. It was built to accomplish a social mission—to make the world more open and connected.

We think it's important that everyone who invests in Facebook understands what this mission means to us, how we make decisions and why we do the things we do. I will try to outline our approach in this letter.

At Facebook, we're inspired by technologies that have revolutionized how people spread and consume information. We often talk about inventions like the printing press and the television—by simply making communication more efficient, they led to a complete transformation of many important parts of society. They gave more people a voice. They encouraged progress. They changed the way society was organized. They brought us closer together.

Today, our society has reached another tipping point. We live at a moment when the majority of people in the world have access to the Internet or mobile phones—the raw tools necessary to start sharing what they're thinking, feeling and doing with whomever they want. Facebook aspires to build the services that give people the power to share and help them once again transform many of our core institutions and industries.

There is a huge need and a huge opportunity to get everyone in the world connected, to give everyone a voice and to help transform society for the future. The scale of the technology and infrastructure that must be built is unprecedented, and we believe this is the most important problem we can focus on.

We hope to strengthen how people relate to each other.

Even if our mission sounds big, it starts small—with the relationship between two people.

Personal relationships are the fundamental unit of our society. Relationships are how we discover new ideas, understand our world and ultimately derive long-term happiness.

At Facebook, we build tools to help people connect with the people they want and share what they want, and by doing this we are extending people's capacity to build and maintain relationships.

People sharing more—even if just with their close friends or families—creates a more open culture and leads to a better understanding of the lives and perspectives of others. We believe that this creates a greater number of stronger relationships between people, and that it helps people get exposed to a greater number of diverse perspectives.

By helping people form these connections, we hope to rewire the way people spread and consume information. We think the world's information infrastructure should resemble the social graph—a network built from the bottom up or peer-to-peer, rather than the monolithic, top-down structure that has existed to date. We also believe that giving people control over what they share is a fundamental principle of this rewiring.

We have already helped more than 800 million people map out more than 100 billion connections so far, and our goal is to help this rewiring accelerate.

We hope to improve how people connect to businesses and the economy.

We think a more open and connected world will help create a stronger economy with more authentic businesses that build better products and services.

As people share more, they have access to more opinions from the people they trust about the products and services they use. This makes it easier to discover the best products and improve the quality and efficiency of their lives.

One result of making it easier to find better products is that businesses will be rewarded for building better products—ones that are personalized and designed around people. We have found that products that are "social by design" tend to be more engaging than their traditional counterparts, and we look forward to seeing more of the world's products move in this direction.

Our developer platform has already enabled hundreds of thousands of businesses to build higher-quality and more social products. We have seen disruptive new approaches in industries like games, music and news, and we expect to see similar disruption in more industries by new approaches that are social by design.

In addition to building better products, a more open world will also encourage businesses to engage with their customers directly and authentically. More than four million businesses have Pages on Facebook that they use to have a dialogue with their customers. We expect this trend to grow as well.

We hope to change how people relate to their governments and social institutions.

We believe building tools to help people share can bring a more honest and transparent dialogue around government that could lead to more direct empowerment of people, more accountability for officials and better solutions to some of the biggest problems of our time.

By giving people the power to share, we are starting to see people make their voices heard on a different scale from what has historically been possible. These voices will increase in number and volume. They cannot be ignored. Over time, we expect governments will become more responsive to issues and concerns raised directly by all their people rather than through intermediaries controlled by a select few.

Through this process, we believe that leaders will emerge across all countries who are pro-Internet and fight for the rights of their people, including the right to share what they want and the right to access all information that people want to share with them.

Finally, as more of the economy moves towards higher-quality products that are personalized, we also expect to see the emergence of new services that are social by design to address the large worldwide problems we face in job creation, education and health care. We look forward to doing what we can to help this progress.

Our Mission and Our Business

As I said above, Facebook was not originally founded to be a company. We've always cared primarily about our social mission, the services we're building and the people who use them. This is a different approach for a public company to take, so I want to explain why I think it works.

I started off by writing the first version of Facebook myself because it was something I wanted to exist. Since then, most of the ideas and code that have gone into Facebook have come from the great people we've attracted to our team.

Most great people care primarily about building and being a part of great things, but they also want to make money. Through the process of building a team—and also building a developer community, advertising market and investor base—I've developed a deep appreciation for how building a strong company with a strong economic engine and strong growth can be the best way to align many people to solve important problems.

Simply put: we don't build services to make money; we make money to build better services.

And we think this is a good way to build something. These days I think more and more people want to use services from companies that believe in something beyond simply maximizing profits.

By focusing on our mission and building great services, we believe we will create the most value for our shareholders and partners over the long term—and this in turn will enable us to keep attracting the best people and building more great services. We don't wake up in the morning with the primary goal of making money, but we understand that the best way to achieve our mission is to build a strong and valuable company.

This is how we think about our IPO as well. We're going public for our employees and our investors. We made a commitment to them when we gave them equity that we'd work hard to make it worth a lot and make it liquid, and this IPO is fulfilling our commitment. As we become a public company, we're making a similar commitment to our new investors and we will work just as hard to fulfill it.

The Hacker Way

As part of building a strong company, we work hard at making Facebook the best place for great people to have a big impact on the world and learn from other great people. We have cultivated a unique culture and management approach that we call the Hacker Way.

The word "hacker" has an unfairly negative connotation from being portrayed in the media as people who break into computers. In reality, hacking just means building something quickly or testing the boundaries of what can be done. Like most things, it can be used for good or bad, but the vast majority of hackers I've met tend to be idealistic people who want to have a positive impact on the world.

The Hacker Way is an approach to building that involves continuous improvement and iteration. Hackers believe that something can always be better, and that nothing is ever complete. They just have to go fix it—often in the face of people who say it's impossible or are content with the status quo.

Hackers try to build the best services over the long term by quickly releasing and learning from smaller iterations rather than trying to get everything right all at once. To support this, we have built a testing framework that at any given time can try out thousands of versions of Facebook. We have the words "Done is better than perfect" painted on our walls to remind ourselves to always keep shipping.

Hacking is also an inherently hands-on and active discipline. Instead of debating for days whether a new idea is possible or what the best way to build something is, hackers would rather just prototype something and see what works. There's a hacker mantra that you'll hear a lot around Facebook offices: "Code wins arguments."

Hacker culture is also extremely open and meritocratic. Hackers believe that the best idea and implementation should always win—not the person who is best at lobbying for an idea or the person who manages the most people.

To encourage this approach, every few months we have a hackathon, where everyone builds prototypes for new ideas they have. At the end, the whole team gets together and looks at everything that has been built. Many of our most successful products came out of hackathons, including Timeline, chat, video, our mobile development framework and some of our most important infrastructure like the HipHop compiler.

To make sure all our engineers share this approach, we require all new engineers—even managers whose primary job will not be to write code—to go through a program called Bootcamp where they learn our codebase, our tools and our approach. There are a lot of folks in the industry who manage engineers and don't want to code themselves, but the type of hands-on people we're looking for are willing and able to go through Bootcamp.

The examples above all relate to engineering, but we have distilled these principles into five core values for how we run Facebook:

Focus on Impact

If we want to have the biggest impact, the best way to do this is to make sure we always focus on solving the most important problems. It sounds simple, but we think most companies do this poorly and waste a lot of time. We expect everyone at Facebook to be good at finding the biggest problems to work on.

Move Fast

Moving fast enables us to build more things and learn faster. However, as most companies grow, they slow down too much because they're more afraid of making mistakes than they are of losing opportunities by moving too slowly. We have a saying: "Move fast and break things." The idea is that if you never break anything, you're probably not moving fast enough.

Be Bold

Building great things means taking risks. This can be scary and prevents most companies from doing the bold things they should. However, in a world that's changing so quickly, you're guaranteed to fail if you don't take any risks. We have another saying: "The riskiest thing is to take no risks." We encourage everyone to make bold decisions, even if that means being wrong some of the time.

Be Open

We believe that a more open world is a better world because people with more information can make better decisions and have a greater impact. That goes for running our company as well. We work hard to make sure everyone at Facebook has access to as much information as possible about every part of the company so they can make the best decisions and have the greatest impact.

Build Social Value

Once again, Facebook exists to make the world more open and connected, and not just to build a company. We expect everyone at Facebook to focus every day on how to build real value for the world in everything they do.

Thanks for taking the time to read this letter. We believe that we have an opportunity to have an important impact on the world and build a lasting company in the process. I look forward to building something great together.

—*United States Securities and Exchange Commission,*
"Form S-1 Registration Statement: Facebook, Inc."
February 1, 2012

MILESTONES

1984

Mark Zuckerberg (MZ) is born in White Plains, New York, on May 14 to Karen and Edward Zuckerberg. (The family later moves to Dobbs Ferry, New York, where he and his sisters were raised. His parents still live there.)

1996

MZ creates Zucknet, a messaging program written in Atari BASIC. It is used by his father, a dentist, at work and also at home.

1998

September: MZ enrolls in Ardsley High School, where he excelled in the classics.

2000

September: MZ enrolls in Phillips Exeter Academy, a prestigious prep school.

2001

Under the company name of Intelligent Media Group, MZ builds a media player called Synapse.

Both AOL and Microsoft try to buy the program, but MZ declines.

2002

June: MZ graduates from Phillips Exeter Academy, where he won prizes in science and classical studies and captained the fencing team.

September: MZ begins first year at Harvard University, where he joins a Jewish fraternity, Alpha Epsilon Pi.

2003

MZ writes CourseMatch, software designed to link Harvard students with the courses they are taking; he also writes Facemash, which juxtaposes photos of female students for users to evaluate who is "hotter."

MZ meets Priscilla Chan at a frat party at Alpha Epsilon Pi.

2004

February 4: Working out of his dormitory room at Harvard with Dustin Moskovitz, Eduardo Saverin, and Chris Hughes, MZ posts the first iteration of Facebook on the Internet: Thefacebook.com. It is available exclusively to the Harvard community.

March: MZ expands reach of his fledgling website to a select few other schools, including Stanford, Columbia, and Yale.

June: MZ drops out of Harvard to further develop his social networking site. He moves to Palo Alto, California, where he and his friends rent a suburban ranch home that doubles as an office.

August: MZ launches Wirehog, a peer-to-peer file sharing service.

September: MZ launches the Facebook Wall.

September: A lawsuit filed by Cameron and Tyler Winklevoss and Divya Narendra claims MZ ripped off the key ideas of the social networking site they were developing (HarvardConnection.com).

Thefacebook hits 1 million users.

2005

May 6: Accel Partners invest $13 million in MZ's company.

May to October: MZ expands the reach of the social network to US colleges, high schools, and international schools.

August: MZ changes the company name to Facebook, after buying the domain name facebook.com for a reported $200,000. (Sean Parker suggested to Mark that he simplify the company name from Thefacebook to Facebook.)

October: Facebook launches a photo sharing service.

Facebook hits 6 million users.

2006

May: Facebook opens up to business networks. Yahoo's offer to buy Facebook for $1 billion is declined.

September: Facebook opens up to anyone 13 years old or older.

December: Facebook hits 12 million users.

2007

March: The lawsuit filed by the Winklevosses and Narendra is dismissed without prejudice, but is subsequently refiled.

May 24: Facebook launches Facebook Platform, for programmers wishing to write social applications.

August: *MIT Technology Review* cites MZ as one of the top 35 innovators under 35.

October: Microsoft's CEO Steve Ballmer offers to buy Facebook for $15 billion. MZ says no. Instead, Microsoft buys a $240 million stake in the company.

Facebook hits 58 million users.

2008

January: MZ wins Techcrunch's Crunchie Award for Best Startup CEO.

June: The Winklevoss/Narendra lawsuit is settled out of court.

Facebook hits 145 million users.

2009

February: Facebook introduces the Like button for use on its own website as well as third-party websites.

December: Facebook hits 360 million users.

2010

July 21: Facebook hits 500 million users.

September: MZ donates $100 million to the Newark, New Jersey, public school system. Priscilla Chan, a medical student, moves into MZ's Palo Alto house, which he rents.

September: *New Statesman* magazine ranks him as number 16 of the world's 50 most influential figures.

October 1: *The Social Network*, a motion picture directed by David Fincher and based on Ben Mezrich's nonfiction book *The Accidental Billionaires*, is released.

October 3: In an episode of *The Simpsons* titled "Loan-a-Lisa," MZ lends his voice to his own cartoon character.

October: *Vanity Fair* ranks MZ as number 1 of the 100 "most influential people of the Information Age."

December: *Time* magazine names MZ Person of the Year.

December: MZ promises to give away half his fortune to charity, joining Microsoft cofounder Bill Gates and investor Warren Buffett in the Giving Pledge.

Facebook hits 608 million users.

2011

Facebook introduces a new feature, Timeline. January 29: Mark appears as a surprise guest on *Saturday Night Live*, as does Jesse Eisenberg who portrayed him in *The Social Network*.

March: Facebook hosts its first worldwide programming competition, the Facebook Hacker Cup.

April 10: MZ announces on his Timeline that Facebook has acquired Instagram.

MZ buys a house for $7 million in Palo Alto, California.

December: Facebook moves to its new corporate offices at 1601 Willow Road, Menlo Park, California. (1 Hacker Way is the address for a ring road around its East Campus.)

2012

May 18: Facebook's initial public offering sells at $38 a share, raising $16 billion for a market cap of $104 billion.

May 19: MZ marries Priscilla Chan, which he announces by posting a "life event" on his Facebook page. (Guests, which numbered fewer than 100, had no inkling they were invited to a wedding. They thought it was a celebratory party for Chan's graduation from medical school.)

June: Facebook hits 955 million users.

October: MZ announces that Facebook hit the 1 billion mark. He remarks, "Well, just everyone came together and counted down. Then we all went back to work."

RECOMMENDED RESOURCES

The Facebook Effect: The Inside Story of the Company That Is Connecting the World, by David Kirkpatrick, is billed as "the real story behind *The Social Network*." It's an important distinction, because *The Social Network* and the book on which it is based are partly fictionalized. In contrast, *The Facebook Effect* is nonfiction, cites its sources, and has an index.

Kirkpatrick explains "Facebook cooperated extensively in the preparation of *The Facebook Effect*, as did CEO Mark Zuckerberg. Almost nobody connected to the company refused to talk to me. However, there was no quid pro quo. Facebook neither requested nor received any rights of approval, and as far as I know, its executives did not see the book before it went to press."

The book is informative, useful, and authoritative—it's the most significant resource for anyone wanting the true story of Facebook and its cofounder, Mark Zuckerberg.

For an insider's look at Facebook's early years, especially its male-centric, tech-oriented corporate culture, *The Boy Kings: A Journey Into the Heart of the Social Network,* by Katherine Losse, is fascinating reading. What emerges is a portrait of a company that held engineers as its high priests, and everyone else—sales, customer support, marketing, managers—as its disciples who were expected to subscribe fully to its mission.

In an interview, Losse, the 51st employee at Facebook, was asked by Kelly Faircloth of betabeat.com about the direction of social media and about privacy concerns. Losse replied, "The reason I wrote the book was to start having a conversation about it. I don't think there is one answer, and I definitely don't think the answer is we're going to go back to the days of only speaking to people face-to-face and completely rejecting social media technology. I think what may happen is social media is going to have to become ever more nuanced and able to capture our real-life relationships, and we're probably just at the first stage of that" (June 27, 2012).

The Accidental Billionaires: The Founding of Facebook, by Harvard graduate Ben Mezrich, is a fictional account of the company. The book is the basis for the critically and financially successful movie, *The Social Network.* Mark Zuckerberg declined to be interviewed for this book.

In his author's note, Mezrich explains, "There are a number of different—and often contentious—opinions about some of the events that took place. Trying to paint a scene from the memories of dozens of sources—some direct witnesses, some indirect—can often lead to discrepancies. I re-created the scenes in the book based on the information I uncovered. . . ."

For that reason, *The Accidental Billionaires* is most useful for getting a sense of Facebook's history; however, readers who want a more factual telling are better served by *The Facebook Effect*.

As with Mezrich's *Bringing Down the House*, which was made into a movie, *The Accidental Billionaires* was also adapted into a film, titled *The Social Network*. Released in 2010 by Columbia Pictures, *The Social Network* gives a great sense of the turbulence Facebook encountered in its early development.

The Social Network garnered eight Academy Award nominations, winning three (Best Adapted Screenplay, Best Original Score, Best Film Editing). At the 68th Golden Globe Awards, it won Best Motion Picture: Drama, Best Director, Best Screenplay, and Best Original Score.

Actor Jesse Eisenberg, in his portrayal of an intense, single-minded, and condescending Mark Zuckerberg, is very convincing—so much so that when he was spotted by a CBS TV news commentator in the bleachers at the London Olympics in

2012, he was erroneously identified as Mark Zuckerberg.

For an overview of Facebook itself, consult *Facebook for Dummies* (4th edition) by Carolyn Abram, *The Complete Idiot's Guide to Facebook* (2nd edition) by Mikal E. Belicove and Joe Kraynak, and *Facebook: The Missing Manual* (3rd edition) by E.A. Vander Veer.

CITATIONS

Personal

Being Robbed

Ellen McGirt, "Facebook's Mark Zuckerberg: Hacker. Dropout. CEO." *Fast Company*, May 1, 2007. http://www.fastcompany.com/59441 /facebooks-mark-zuckerberg-hacker-dropout-ceo

Eliminating Desire

Lev Grossman, "2010 Person of the Year: Mark Zuckerberg," *Time*, December 27, 2010/January 3, 2011. http://www.time.com/time/specials /packages/article/0,28804,2036683_2037183,00 .html

Advice to Students: Get With the Program

Charlie Rose, "Facebook: Charlie Rose interviews Mark Zuckerberg & Sheryl Sandberg," *Charlie Rose*, recorded at Facebook's offices in Palo Alto, Ca., November 7, 2011. http://www.charlierose .com/view/interview/11981

Google+ Profile

Chris Gayomali, "The Most Followed Person on Google+ is Mark Zuckerberg," *Time*: Techland, July 5, 2011. http://techland.time.com/2011/07/05/ the-most-followed-person-on-google-is-mark -zuckerberg

Getting Zucked

Leslie Stahl, "The Face behind Facebook," *60 Minutes*, January 13, 2008. http://www.cbsnews.com /video/watch/?id=3706601n

Death Sentence

Guy Raz, "Net@40: The Facebook Effect," Computer History Museum, July 21, 2010. http://www .computerhistory.org/events/video/?videoid =_TuFkupUn7k

Speaking Mandarin

Patricia Sellers, "Mark Zuckerberg's New Challenge," *Fortune*: Postcards, May 26, 2011. http:// postcards.blogs.fortune.cnn.com/2011/05/26/mark -zuckerbergs-new-challenge-eating-only-what-he -kills

Embracing *The Lord of the Flies*

Patricia Sellers, "Mark Zuckerberg's Facebook Comment on Eating Only What He Kills," *Fortune*: Postcards, May 27, 2011. http://postcards.blogs .fortune.cnn.com/2011/05/27/mark-zuckerbergs -facebook-comment-on-eating-only-what-he-kills/

Focus and Simplicity

PBS, "Facebook: Charlie Rose interviews Mark Zuckerberg & Sheryl Sandberg," *Charlie Rose*, recorded at Facebook's offices in Palo Alto, Ca., November 7, 2011. http://www.charlierose.com /view/interview/11981

Zuckerberg's Likes

"Blackboard: Mark Zuckerberg," *Business Insider*. http://www.businessinsider.com/blackboard /mark-zuckerberg

College

Mindset

Nicholas Carlson, "Exclusive: How Mark Zuckerberg Booted His Co-Founder Out Of The Company," *Business Insider*. http://articles .businessinsider.com/2012-05-15 /tech/31706573_1_ceo-mark-zuckerberg -billionaire-facebook-eduardo-saverin

Animal Farm

"It's Facebook's Birthday! Anniversary Marks The Site's Sixth Year," *Huffington Post*, April 5, 2010. http://www.huffingtonpost.com/2010/02/03 /facebook-birthday-anniver_n_447972.html

No Job

Michael M. Grynbaum, "Mark E. Zuckerberg '06: The Whiz Behind Thefacebook.com," *Harvard Crimson*, June 10, 2004. http://www.thecrimson .com/article/2004/6/10/mark-e-zuckerberg-06-the -whiz

HarvardConnection

Nicholas Carlson, "At Last—The Full Story of How Facebook Was Founded," *Business Insider*, March 5, 2010. http://www.businessinsider.com/how -facebook-was-founded-2010-3?op=1

Hacking for the Fun of It

Michael M. Grynbaum, "Mark E. Zuckerberg '06: The Whiz Behind Thefacebook.com," *Harvard Crimson*, June 10, 2004. http://www.thecrimson .com/article/2004/6/10/mark-e-zuckerberg-06-the -whiz

Building Thefacebook

Leslie Stahl, "Mark Zuckerberg & Facebook," *60 Minutes*, December 1, 2010. http://www.cbsnews .com/video/watch/?id=7120522n

Zuckerberg's Initial Debt

Noah Robischon, "Young Mark Zuckerberg on Film: 'We Ran The Site Originally for $85 a Month,'" *Fast Company*, July 28, 2009. http:// www.fastcompany.com/1319242 /young-mark-zuckerberg-film-we-ran-site -originally-85-month

Code Monkey

Henry Blodget, "Mark Zuckerberg, Moving Fast and Breaking Things," *Business Insider*, October 14, 2010. http://www.businessinsider.com /mark-zuckerberg-2010-10

Backing Out of HarvardConnection

Nicholas Carlson, "At Last—The Full Story Of How Facebook Was Founded," *Business Insider*, March 5, 2010. http://www.businessinsider.com /how-facebook-was-founded-2010-3?op=1

Psychology + CS = Facebook

Lev Grossman, "2010 Person of the Year: Mark Zuckerberg," *Time*, December 27, 2010/January 3, 2011. http://www.time.com/time/specials /packages/article/0,28804,2036683_2037183,00 .html

Maturation

Kara Swisher, "Full D8 Interview Video: Facebook CEO Mark Zuckerberg," *All Things D*, June 10, 2010. http://allthingsd.com/20100610/full-d8 -video-facebook-ceo-mark-zuckerberg

Facebook's Origin

Adam L. Penenberg, "Exclusive Interview: Facebook's Mark Zuckerberg on the Value of Viral Loops," *Fast Company*, September 17, 2009. http://www.fastcompany.com/1361224/exclusive-interview-facebooks-mark-zuckerberg-value-viral-loops

Jettisoning Eduardo Saverin

Nicholas Carlson, "Exclusive: How Mark Zuckerberg Booted His Co-Founder Out Of The Company," *Business Insider*. http://articles.businessinsider.com/2012-05-15/tech/31706573_1_ceo-mark-zuckerberg-billionaire-facebook-eduardo-saverin

Stock Dilution of Saverin's Shares

Nicholas Carlson, "Exclusive: Here's the Email Zuckerberg Sent to Cut His Cofounder Out of Facebook," Business Insider, May 15, 2012. http://www.businessinsider.com/exclusive-heres-the-email-zuckerberg-sent-to-cut-his-cofounder-out-of-facebook-2012-5

Starting Out

Silicon Valley's Culture

Jessica Livingston, "2011 Startup School Q&A with Mark Zuckerberg," Startup School, October 29, 2011. http://www.youtube.com/watch?v=XXlcYosCRgw

Location, Location, Location

Network World, "Facebook CEO Mark Zuckerberg's Remarks at MIT," November 8, 2011. http://www.youtube.com/watch?v=4c2_VOJ4ryI

Silicon Valley's Short-Term Vision

Jessica Livingston, "2011 Startup School Q&A with Mark Zuckerberg," Startup School, October 29, 2011. http://www.youtube.com/watch?v=XXlcYosCRgw

Dumb Mistakes

Jessica Livingston, "2011 Startup School Q&A with Mark Zuckerberg," Startup School, October 29, 2011. http://www.youtube.com/watch?v=XXlcYosCRgw

MySpace and Facebook: Cool vs. Useful

Guy Raz, "Net@40: The Facebook Effect," Computer History Museum, July 21, 2010. http://www.computerhistory.org/events/video/?videoid=_TuFkupUn7k

Facebook

Mission-Oriented

Jose Antonio Vargas, "Our Facebook—Led by Mark Zuckerberg, We Define an Era," *Huffington Post*, May 14, 2012. http://www.huffingtonpost.com/jose-antonio-vargas/facebook-ipo-mark-zuckerberg_b_1514931.html

Independence

Laura Locke, "The Future of Facebook," *Time*, July 17, 2007. http://www.time.com/time/business /article/0,8599,1644040,00.html

Corporate Culture

Dan Fletcher, "Q&A With Facebook CEO Mark Zuckerberg," *Time*, May 27, 2010. http://newsfeed .time.com/2010/05/27/times-qa-with-facebook -ceo-mark-zuckerberg

Board, Not Bored, Meetings

"How Do You Prep for a Board Meeting?" *Fast Company*: 30 Second MBA. http://www .fastcompany.com/mba/question/how-do-you -prep-board-meeting

Core Desire

Charlie Rose, "Facebook: Charlie Rose interviews Mark Zuckerberg & Sheryl Sandberg," *Charlie Rose*, recorded at Facebook's offices in Palo Alto, Ca., November 7, 2011. http://www.charlierose .com/view/interview/11981

Core Principles

"From Facebook, Answering Privacy Concerns with New Settings," *Washington Post*, May 24, 2010. http://www.washingtonpost.com/wp-dyn /content/article/2010/05/23/AR2010052303828 .html

Reach

Diane Sawyer, "Facebook CEO Mark Zuckerberg Talks to Diane Sawyer as Website Gets 500-Millionth Member," *ABC World News*, recorded at Facebook's offices in Palo Alto, Ca., July 21, 2010. http://abcnews.go.com/WN/zuckerberg-calls -movie-fiction-disputes-signing-contract-giving /story?id=11217015#.UGoObhxoj8M

Education

Startup: Education, "Blog Post from Mark Zuckerberg," Facebook, September 24, 2010. http://www .facebook.com/notes/startup-education/blog-post -from-mark-zuckerberg/116078918450633

Goals

Michael M. Grynbaum, "Mark E. Zuckerberg '06: The Whiz Behind Thefacebook.com," *Harvard Crimson*, June 10, 2004. http://www.thecrimson .com/article/2004/6/10/mark-e-zuckerberg -06-the-whiz

Instagram

"Facebook to Acquire Instagram," Facebook press release, April 9, 2012. https://www.facebook.com /zuck/posts/10100318398827991

Lawyers

Evelyn M. Rusli, Nicole Perlroth, and Nick Bilton, "The Education of Mark Zuckerberg," *New York Times*, May 12, 2012. http://www.nytimes.com/2012/05/13/technology/facebooks-mark-zuckerberg-at-a-turning-point.html?pagewanted=all&_r=0

Mobile Platforms

"Facebook Management Discusses Q2 2012 Results-Earnings Call Transcript," Seeking Alpha, July 26, 2012. http://seekingalpha.com/article/755071-facebook-management-discusses-q2-2012-results-earnings-call-transcript

News Feed

"Calm down. Breathe. We Hear You," Facebook Blog, September 5, 2006. http://blog.facebook.com/blog.php?post=2208197130

In Touch

Guy Raz, "Net@40: The Facebook Effect," Computer History Museum, July 21, 2010. http://www.computerhistory.org/events/video/?videoid=_TuFkupUn7k

Online Directory

James Breyer, "From Harvard to the Facebook," Entrepreneurial Thought Leaders Seminars, Stanford Center for Professional Development, MS&E 472, Autumn Quarter, 2005. http://ecorner .stanford.edu/authorMaterialInfo.html?mid=1567

Openness

James Breyer, "From Harvard to the Facebook," Entrepreneurial Thought Leaders Seminars, Stanford Center for Professional Development, MS&E 472, Autumn Quarter, 2005. http://ecorner .stanford.edu/authorMaterialInfo.html?mid=1567

People-Centric

"Now Connecting 250 Million People," Facebook Blog, July 15, 2009. http://blog.facebook.com/blog .php?post=106860717130

Connecting

"Six Years of Making Connections," Facebook Blog, February 4, 2010. http://blog.facebook.com /blog.php?post=287542162130

Information Control

"On Facebook, People Own and Control Their Information," Facebook Blog, February 16, 2009. http://blog.facebook.com/blog .php?post=54434097130

Sharing

Kara Swisher, "The Entire D6 Interview With Facebook's Mark Zuckerberg and Sheryl Sandberg," *All Things D*, May 28, 2008. http://allthingsd.com/20080818/the-entire-d6-interview-with-facebooks-mark-zuckerberg-and-sheryl-sandberg-1-of-4/

Privacy

"From Facebook, Answering Privacy Concerns with New Settings," *Washington Post*, May 24, 2010. http://www.washingtonpost.com/wp-dyn/content/article/2010/05/23/AR2010052303828.html

Privacy Settings

"From Facebook, Answering Privacy Concerns with New Settings," *Washington Post*, May 24, 2010. http://www.washingtonpost.com/wp-dyn/content/article/2010/05/23/AR2010052303828.html

Privacy Tools

Charlie Rose, "Facebook: Charlie Rose interviews Mark Zuckerberg & Sheryl Sandberg," *Charlie Rose*, recorded at Facebook's offices in Palo Alto, Ca., November 7, 2011. http://www.charlierose.com/view/interview/11981

Privacy from Day One

"Our Commitment to the Facebook Community," Facebook Blog, November 29, 2011. http://blog .facebook.com/blog.php?post=10150378701937131

Sharing Information

Charlie Rose, "Facebook: Charlie Rose interviews Mark Zuckerberg & Sheryl Sandberg," *Charlie Rose*, recorded at Facebook's offices in Palo Alto, Ca., November 7, 2011. http://www.charlierose .com/view/interview/11981

Self-Revelations

Charlie Rose, "Facebook: Charlie Rose interviews Mark Zuckerberg & Sheryl Sandberg," *Charlie Rose*, recorded at Facebook's offices in Palo Alto, Ca., November 7, 2011. http://www.charlierose .com/view/interview/11981

Information Conduit

"200 Million Strong," Facebook Blog, April 8, 2009. http://blog.facebook.com/blog.php?post =72353897130

Virtual Friends, Virtually Forever

Lev Grossman, "2010 Person of the Year: Mark Zuckerberg," *Time*, December 27, 2010/January 3, 2011. http://www.time.com/time/specials /packages/article/0,28804,2036683_2037183,00 .html

The Super Power of Word of Mouth

Adam L. Penenberg, "Exclusive Interview: Facebook's Mark Zuckerberg on the Value of Viral Loops," *Fast Company*, September 17, 2009. http://www.fastcompany.com/1361224/exclusive-interview-facebooks-mark-zuckerberg-value-viral-loops

Lawsuits

Every Capitalist

Email to Harvard dean John Walsh, February 17, 2004. http://pdf.edocr.com/a31f6559ca7795f33904ec6ffc1fb732598fde16.pdf

I Fought the Law and the Law Won

Leslie Stahl, "Mark Zuckerberg & Facebook," *60 Minutes*, December 1, 2010. http://www.cbsnews.com/8301-18560_162-7108060/mark-zuckerberg-and-facebook-whats-next/?pageNum=7&tag=contentMain;contentBody

Big Brother Is Watching

"Our Commitment to the Facebook Community," Facebook Blog, November 29, 2011. http://blog.facebook.com/blog.php?post=10150378701937131

The Social Network

The Social Network

Ki Mae Heussner, "Facebook's Zuckerberg Shows Softer Side to Oprah," *ABC News*, September 24, 2010. Posted online January 24, 2011. http://abc news.go.com/Technology/facebooks -zuckerberg-announces-100m-donation-schools -oprah/story?id=11718356#.UG5SZK7-1t1

The Social Network's Depiction of Zuckerberg

Perri Nemiroff, "Mark Zuckerberg on What The Social Network Got Right and Wrong," Moviefone, October 19, 2010. http://blog.moviefone .com/2010/10/19/mark-zuckerberg-the-social -network

The Social Network's Positive Aspects

Leslie Stahl, "Mark Zuckerberg & Facebook," *60 Minutes*, December 1, 2010. http://www.cbsnews .com/video/watch/?id=7120522n

Mission

Ubiquity

Charlie Rose, "Facebook: Charlie Rose interviews Mark Zuckerberg & Sheryl Sandberg," *Charlie Rose*, recorded at Facebook's offices in Palo Alto, Ca., November 7, 2011. http://www.charlierose .com/view/interview/11981

Long-Range Vision

Ellen McGirt, "Facebook's Mark Zuckerberg: Hacker. Dropout. CEO." *Fast Company*, May 1, 2007. http://www.fastcompany.com/59441 /facebooks-mark-zuckerberg-hacker-dropout-ceo

Steve Jobs

Charlie Rose, "Facebook: Charlie Rose interviews Mark Zuckerberg & Sheryl Sandberg," *Charlie Rose*, recorded at Facebook's offices in Palo Alto, Ca., November 7, 2011. http://www.charlierose .com/view/interview/11981

Process

Product Improvement

Ellen McGirt, "'Boy CEO' Mark Zuckerberg's Two Smartest Projects Were Growing Facebook And Growing Up," *Fast Company*, March 19, 2012. http://www.fastcompany.com/1822794/boy -ceo-mark-zuckerbergs-two-smartest-projects -were-growing-facebook-and-growing

On Innovation

"How do you generate innovation?" *Fast Company*: 30 Second MBA. http://www.fastcompany .com/mba/profile/mark-zuckerberg

On Focus

E.B. Boyd, "Mark Zuckerberg, Nonplussed by Google, Sets Facebook's New Course," *Fast Company*, July 6, 2011. http://www.fastcompany .com/1765371/mark-zuckerberg-nonplussed -google-sets-facebooks-new-course

Social Context and Serendipity

Lev Grossman, "2010 Person of the Year: Mark Zuckerberg," *Time*, December 27, 2010/January 3, 2011. http://www.time.com/time/specials /packages/article/0,28804,2036683_2037183,00 .html

First Things First

Charlie Rose, "Facebook: Charlie Rose interviews Mark Zuckerberg & Sheryl Sandberg," *Charlie Rose*, recorded at Facebook's offices in Palo Alto, Ca., November 7, 2011. http://www.charlierose .com/view/interview/11981

Fast Movers

Henry Blodget, "Mark Zuckerberg, Moving Fast and Breaking Things," *Business Insider*, October 14, 2010. http://www.businessinsider.com /mark-zuckerberg-2010-10

The Hacker's Way

Ellen McGirt, "'Boy CEO' Mark Zuckerberg's Two Smartest Projects Were Growing Facebook And Growing Up," *Fast Company*, March 19, 2012. http://www.fastcompany.com/1822794/boy -ceo-mark-zuckerbergs-two-smartest-projects -were-growing-facebook-and-growing

Hacking's Good

Leslie Stahl, "Mark Zuckerberg & Facebook," *60 Minutes*, December 1, 2010. http://www .cbsnews.com/video/watch/?id=7120522n

Hackathons

Henry Blodget, "Mark Zuckerberg, Moving Fast and Breaking Things," *Business Insider*, October 14, 2010. http://www.businessinsider.com/mark -zuckerberg-2010-10

Values

No Games

Charlie Rose, "Facebook: Charlie Rose interviews Mark Zuckerberg & Sheryl Sandberg," *Charlie Rose*, recorded at Facebook's offices in Palo Alto, Ca., November 7, 2011. http://www.charlierose .com/view/interview/11981

Making Mistakes

Ellen McGirt, "'Boy CEO' Mark Zuckerberg's Two Smartest Projects Were Growing Facebook And Growing Up," *Fast Company*, March 19, 2012. http://www.fastcompany.com/1822794/boy-ceo -mark-zuckerbergs-two-smartest-projects-were -growing-facebook-and-growing

Getting Things Done

Ellen McGirt, "Facebook's Mark Zuckerberg: Hacker. Dropout. CEO." *Fast Company*, May 1, 2007. http://www.fastcompany.com/59441 /facebooks-mark-zuckerberg-hacker-dropout-ceo

Siding with the Underdog

Austin Carr, "Facebook Friends an 'Underdog,' Microsoft," *Fast Company*, October 14, 2010. http://www.fastcompany.com/1694882/facebook -friends-underdog-microsoft

Caring

Lev Grossman, "2010 Person of the Year: Mark Zuckerberg," *Time*, December 27, 2010/January 3, 2011. http://www.time.com/time/specials /packages/article/0,28804,2036683_2037183,00.html

Users' Privacy Controls

Dan Fletcher, "How Facebook is Redefining Privacy," *Time*, May 20, 2010. http://www.time.com /time/magazine/article/0,9171,1990798,00.html

Entrepreneur/CEO

Guy Raz, "Net@40: The Facebook Effect," Computer History Museum, July 21, 2010. http://www.computerhistory.org/events/video/?videoid=_TuFkupUn7k

Not Selling Out

Press conference transcribed by David Kirkpatrick, "Zuck: I Could Have Sold Facebook for $1 Billion at Age 22, So No, Revenues Are Not My Top Concern," *Business Insider*, May 28, 2010. http://articles.businessinsider.com/2010-05-28/tech/29963929_1_privacy-yahoo-business-model

Employees' Leverage

"Facebook Management Discusses Q2 2012 Results-Earnings Call Transcript," Seeking Alpha, July 26, 2012. http://seekingalpha.com/article/755071-facebook-management-discusses-q2-2012-results-earnings-call-transcript

The Power of Focus

Kara Swisher, "Full D8 Interview Video: Facebook CEO Mark Zuckerberg," *All Things D*, June 10, 2010. http://allthingsd.com/20100610/full-d8-video-facebook-ceo-mark-zuckerberg

Creating Value

Rick Stengel, "An Interview with Mark Zuckerberg," *Time*, conducted at Facebook's offices in Palo Alto, Ca., 2010. http://www.time.com/time/specials/packages/article/0,28804,2036683_2037109,00.html

Employees Growing on the Job

Jessica Livingston, "2011 Startup School Q&A with Mark Zuckerberg," Startup School, October 29, 2011. http://www.youtube.com/watch?v=XXlcYosCRgw

Measuring Value

Guy Raz, "Net@40: The Facebook Effect," Computer History Museum, July 21, 2010. http://www.computerhistory.org/events/video/?videoid=_TuFkupUn7k

Building Companies

Jessica Livingston, "2011 Startup School Q&A with Mark Zuckerberg," Startup School, October 29, 2011. http://www.youtube.com/watch?v=XXlcYosCRgw

Facebook's Biggest Challenges

James Breyer, "From Harvard to the Facebook," Entrepreneurial Thought Leaders Seminars, Stanford Center for Professional Development, MS&E 472, Autumn Quarter, 2005. http://ecorner.stanford.edu/authorMaterialInfo.html?mid=1567

Prioritizing

James Breyer, "From Harvard to the Facebook," Entrepreneurial Thought Leaders Seminars, Stanford Center for Professional Development, MS&E 472, Autumn Quarter, 2005. http://ecorner .stanford.edu/authorMaterialInfo.html?mid=1567

Hiring Employees

James Breyer, "From Harvard to the Facebook," Entrepreneurial Thought Leaders Seminars, Stanford Center for Professional Development, MS&E 472, Autumn Quarter, 2005. http://ecorner .stanford.edu/authorMaterialInfo.html?mid=1567

Motivation

Laura Locke, "The Future of Facebook," *Time*, July 17, 2007. http://www.time.com/time/business /article/0,8599,1644040,00.html

The Next Big Thing

Michael M. Grynbaum, "Mark E. Zuckerberg '06: The Whiz Behind Thefacebook.com," *Harvard Crimson*, June 10, 2004. http://www.thecrimson .com/article/2004/6/10/mark-e-zuckerberg -06-the-whiz

Fast and Faster

Diane Sawyer, "Facebook CEO Mark Zuckerberg Talks to Diane Sawyer as Website Gets 500-Millionth Member," *ABC World News*, recorded at Facebook's offices in Palo Alto, Ca., July 21, 2010. http://abcnews.go.com/WN/zuckerberg-calls -movie-fiction-disputes-signing-contract-giving /story?id=11217015#.UGoObhxoj8M

Selling Out

Evelyn M. Rusli, Nicole Perlroth, and Nick Bilton, "The Education of Mark Zuckerberg," *New York Times*, May 12, 2012. http://www.nytimes .com/2012/05/13/technology/face books-mark-zuckerberg-at-a-turning-point .html?pagewanted=all&_r=0

Accountability

Stepping In It and Scraping It Off

"An Open Letter from Mark Zuckerberg," Facebook Blog, September 8, 2006. http://blog .facebook.com/blog.php?post=2208562130

On FTC Allegations of Privacy Violations

"Our Commitment to the Facebook Community," Facebook Blog, November 29, 2011. http://blog .facebook.com/blog.php?post=10150378701937131

Vision

SOPA (Stop Online Piracy) and PIPA (Protect Intellectual Property Act)

"The Internet Is the Most Powerful . . . ," Facebook Blog, January 18, 2012. http://www.facebook.com /zuck/posts/10100210345757211

A Blinding Flash of the Obvious

Jose Antonio Vargas, "Letter from Palo Alto: The Face of Facebook," *New Yorker*, September 20, 2010. http://www.newyorker.com /reporting/2010/09/20/100920fa_fact_vargas

On the Future of Email

Austin Carr, "Facebook Friends an 'Underdog,' Microsoft," *Fast Company*, October 14, 2010. http://www.fastcompany.com/1694882/facebook -friends-underdog-microsoft

Risk-Taking

Jessica Livingston, "2011 Startup School Q&A with Mark Zuckerberg," Startup School, October 29, 2011. http://www.youtube.com /watch?v=XXlcYosCRgw

Facebook's Future

Guy Raz, "Net@40: The Facebook Effect," Computer History Museum, July 21, 2010. http://www .computerhistory.org/events/video/?videoid =_TuFkupUn7k

Social Trending

Guy Raz, "Net@40: The Facebook Effect," Computer History Museum, July 21, 2010. http://www.computerhistory.org/events/video/?videoid=_TuFkupUn7k

The Evolution of Mass Communication Tools

Charlie Rose, "Facebook: Charlie Rose interviews Mark Zuckerberg & Sheryl Sandberg," *Charlie Rose*, recorded at Facebook's offices in Palo Alto, Ca., November 7, 2011. http://www.charlierose.com/view/interview/11981

Responsible Governments

Charlie Rose, "Facebook: Charlie Rose interviews Mark Zuckerberg & Sheryl Sandberg," *Charlie Rose*, recorded at Facebook's offices in Palo Alto, Ca., November 7, 2011. http://www.charlierose.com/view/interview/11981

A Social Web

Dan Fletcher, "How Facebook is Redefining Privacy," *Time*, May 20, 2010. http://www.time.com/time/magazine/article/0,9171,1990798,00.html

Responsibilities

Kara Swisher, "The Entire D6 Interview With Facebook's Mark Zuckerberg and Sheryl Sandberg," *All Things D*, May 28, 2008. http://allthingsd.com/20080818/the-entire-d6-interview-with-facebooks-mark-zuckerberg-and-sheryl-sandberg-1-of-4/

Information Sharing

Saul Hansell, "Zuckerberg's Law of Information Sharing," *New York Times*, November 6, 2008. http://bits.blogs.nytimes.com/2008/11/06/zuckerbergs-law-of-information-sharing

Companies Admired

Shayndi Raice, "Is Facebook Ready for the Big Time?" *Wall Street Journal*, January 14, 2012. http://online.wsj.com/article/SB10001424052970204542404577157113178985408.html

Transparency in History

"Governing the Facebook Service in an Open and Transparent Way," Facebook Blog, February 26, 2009. http://blog.facebook.com/blog.php?post=56566967130

Monetizing: Cash In by Cashing Out

James Breyer, "From Harvard to the Facebook," Entrepreneurial Thought Leaders Seminars, Stanford Center for Professional Development, MS&E 472, Autumn Quarter, 2005. http://ecorner .stanford.edu/authorMaterialInfo.html?mid=1567

The Web's Future

"Building the Social Web Together," Facebook Blog, April 21, 2010. http://blog.facebook.com /blog.php?post=383404517130

On the Future of Social Networking

Lev Grossman, "2010 Person of the Year: Mark Zuckerberg," *Time*, December 27, 2010/January 3, 2011. http://www.time.com/time/specials /packages/article/0,28804,2036683_2037183,00 .html

Philanthropy

Early Philanthropy

Rick Stengel, "An Interview with Mark Zuckerberg," *Time*, conducted at Facebook's offices in Palo Alto, Ca., 2010. http://www .time.com/time/specials/packages /article/0,28804,2036683_2037109,00.html

Organ Donations

Russell Goldman, "Zuckerberg's Dinners with Girl-friend Help Spur Life-Saving Facebook Tool," *ABC News*, May 1, 2012. http://abcnews.go.com/blogs /headlines/2012/05/zuckerbergs-dinners-with -girlfriend-help-spur-life-saving-facebook-tool

The Power of Friends

"Organ Donation: Friends Saving Lives," *ABC News*, May 2, 2012. http://abcnews.go.com /Technology/facebooks-mark-zuckerberg -sheryl-sandberg-facebook-organ-donation /story?id=16247416

ENDNOTES

1. Peter Steiner, "On the Internet, Nobody Knows You're a Dog," *New Yorker* cartoon. July 5, 1993, p. 61.

2. Diane Alter, "Facebook Stock Hits New Low, So What Now for Mark Zuckerberg?" Money Morning, August 17, 2012. http://moneymorning .com/2012/08/17/facebook-stock-hits-new-low -so-what-now-for-mark-zuckerberg/

3. "Facebook: About." https://www.facebook.com /facebook/info

4. Yann Balotelli, "MySpace Is Back: A New Look at an Old Friend," AllMediaNY, October 1, 2012. http://www.allmediany.com/news/6037-myspace -is-back-a-new-look-at-an-old-friend

5. Nigam Arora, "Rupert Murdoch Is Nobody To Tweet About Facebook," *Forbes*, January 20, 2012. http://www.forbes.com/sites/greatspecula- tions/2012/01/30/rupert-murdoch-is-nobody-to -tweet-about-facebook/

6. Julianne Pepitone, "Facebook Wants Court to Dismiss Ceglia Lawsuit," CNNMoney, March 26, 2012. http://money.cnn.com/2012/03/26 /technology/facebook-ceglia-motion-to -dismiss/index.htm

7. Gillian Reagan, "The Evolution of Facebook's Mission Statement," *New York Observer*, July 12, 2009. http://observer.com/2009/07/the-evolution -of-facebooks-mission-statement

ABOUT THE EDITOR

George Beahm, the editor of the internationally bestselling *I, Steve: Steve Jobs In His Own Words*, is a former Army major who served on active duty, in the National Guard, and in the Army Reserves. He has published 35 nonfiction books. Beahm lives in Williamsburg, Virginia. His website is www.georgebeahm.com.